WORTH THE WRESTLE

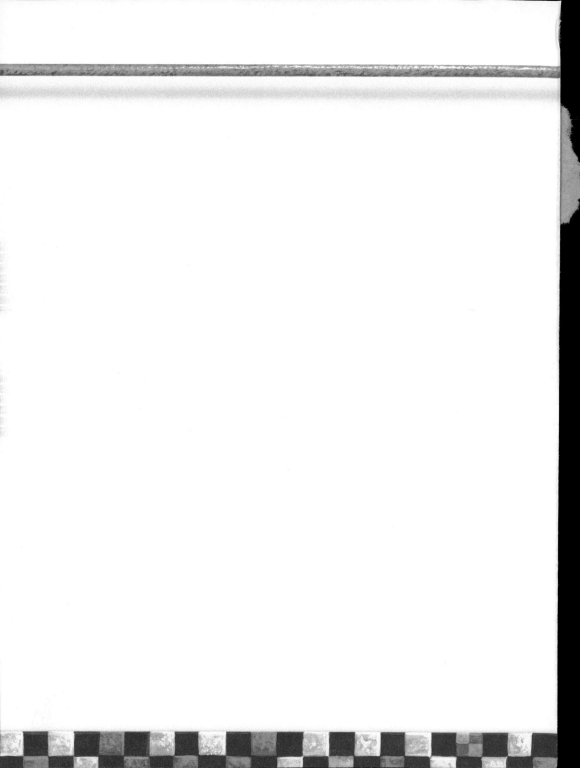

WORTH THE WRESTLE

SHERI DEW

Illustrations by James C. Christensen

DESERET BOOK

Salt Lake City, Utah

Library of Congress Cataloging-in-Publication Data

Names: Dew, Sheri L., author.
Title: Worth the wrestle / Sheri Dew.
Description: Salt Lake City, Utah : Deseret Book, [2017] | Includes bibliographical references.
Identifiers: LCCN 2017000048 | ISBN 9781629722351 (hardbound : alk. paper)
Subjects: LCSH: Christian life—Mormon authors. | Mormons—Religious life. | Faith. | Conversion—The Church of Jesus Christ of Latter-day Saints. | Conversion—Mormon Church.
Classification: LCC BX8656 .D495 2017 | DDC 248.4/89332—dc23
LC record available at https://lccn.loc.gov/2017000048

Printed in the United States of America
Publishers Printing, Salt Lake City, UT

10 9 8 7 6 5 4 3 2 1

To Cathy Chamberlain and James C. Christensen
Two friends whose lives and work
epitomized a joyful wrestle

CONTENTS

INTRODUCTION

In my early twenties, I was a graduate student in history at BYU. My emphasis was on Church history, and one of the courses focused on complex issues in our recorded history. The class was small—fewer than ten students—and most were doctoral candidates, though I was seeking a master's degree.

The professor structured the course so that we spent two weeks discussing a given "problem area" in our history, such as the different recorded versions of the First Vision, or Hawn's Mill, or the Mountain Meadows Massacre. One week we would be assigned to digest a large reading list on the chosen topic, and the following week we would meet to discuss what we had read. I was young and naïve and thought nothing of it when, in the first class period, the professor said, "If any of you are struggling with your testimonies, you may not want to continue with this course." Having been raised in a devout LDS family, I remember thinking, "Well, nothing will bother me."

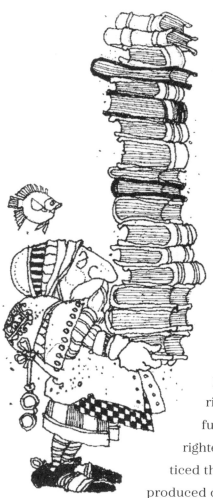

So I dismissed his comment and didn't think about it again—until the day we met to discuss the topic of study for that week: polygamy. I walked into class that day to find an elderly woman seated at the table where we always spread out the stacks of reading material we'd digested. (Remember, this was well before the digital age, back when university students lugged books around.) The table was piled high with books, letters, documents, certificates, family history records, and so forth.

This woman, as it turned out, was the matriarch in a large polygamous family living in southern Utah. The professor turned our several-hour class period over to her, and she proceeded to lay out the premise for the continuation of plural marriage beyond the Manifesto in 1890—with her fundamental argument being that the most righteous of the Lord's people on earth still practiced that law. As she made her case, this woman produced document after document supporting her claims. Any questions I asked that day fell flat. Neither I nor even my more advanced classmates knew enough to debate the issue with her.

I left that class bewildered. To this day, I could walk to the spot on campus where I was standing when I asked myself, "Could she possibly be right?" Her message didn't *feel* right, but her story and argument were convincing—especially for an inexperienced young adult seeing for the first time materials like the ones she'd presented. At that moment, all I knew was that I did not know enough to refute her claims and that her assertions seemed valid.

It was troubling, and I found myself thinking about that experience again and again. Unlike today, at that time it was difficult if not almost impossible for a university student to have access to historical records that would sufficiently address the subject. Very little that was helpful had been written about it. And no one I talked to had answers that were the least bit comforting. So an element of uncertainty gnawed at me, sort of like a leaky faucet dripping in the background. The most unsettling thing was that I found myself wondering what else I didn't know or understand about our history. My testimony wasn't in jeopardy, but I felt stuck spiritually.

In time I finished my course work at BYU and accepted a position as an editor-in-training with a publishing house in Salt Lake City. Two important privileges, even blessings, came to me through that job. First, I worked under the mentorship of a distinguished editor, a gracious and learned man from Great Britain, H. George Bickerstaff. George was a brilliant, meticulous editor, and I watched and learned from him as he worked with some of the brightest minds in our culture to produce classic literary works. One of the major things he taught me was that in the pursuit of a stronger, better, clearer manuscript, a great editor asks great questions. The better and tougher the questions, the more refined the finished product would be.

The second blessing came when George assigned me to work with Truman Madsen as the editor of his biography on Elder B. H. Roberts. Truman was a world-renowned philosopher/scholar and a devout student and superb teacher of the gospel, and I was overwhelmed with the assignment. Truman Madsen was . . . well, Truman Madsen. He was a hero of mine. I resonated with his teachings about the Prophet Joseph Smith and had listened to his talks about the Prophet again and again. Truman's combination of intellect, experience, and spiritual acuity was remarkable, and I wondered what possibly qualified me to attempt to refine his work, as editors do. But I quickly learned that he wanted—no, he expected—me to grill him on anything and everything in his manuscript that raised even the slightest question in my mind. Many times, when I posed those questions, he would respond, "Well, what do *you* think?" What I thought was that *he* was Truman Madsen, that I was a young, lowly, junior editor, and that his opinion mattered infinitely more than did mine. But that wasn't how he saw it—or, at least, that wasn't how he treated me.

Throughout the editing process, Truman and I spent hours discussing possible refinements to his work. As a result, I had the chance to ask this gifted man anything I wanted to ask him—including about polygamy.

Finally there was someone I trusted who was willing to discuss the questions I had on that topic. His specific answers aren't relevant here; what matters is that from him I learned that questions can be instruments of growth. I learned that the Lord will respond to sincere questions. I learned that the humility that accompanies the asking of questions mirrors, though in small measure, the humility demonstrated by the Savior again and again. And I learned that, although there are some answers we don't have, there is no question or issue or problem that the Lord doesn't understand completely, omnipotently.

I wish my history professor had not positioned questions about our history or doctrine as threats to testimony. I'm grateful that George Bickerstaff and Truman Madsen overturned that fear and misperception by teaching me to welcome honest questions. From them I learned that *questions are good*—and that questions asked against a backdrop of faith and with an earnest desire to learn always lead to spiritual growth and a stronger testimony. I remember the moment when, after an editorial session with Truman in which we had discussed some thorny issues, I said to myself, "If someone like Truman Madsen, a philosopher trained to ask the most compelling questions about the meaning of life, can find the answers to his questions in the gospel of Jesus Christ, then surely I can."

Perhaps most of all, I learned from Truman and George that questions are good *as long as* the focus remains on the reality of Jesus Christ as our Savior. For "he manifesteth himself unto all those who believe in him, by the power of the Holy Ghost; yea, unto every nation, kindred, tongue, and people, working mighty miracles, signs, and wonders, among the children of men according to their faith" (2 Nephi 26:13).

CHAPTER 1

QUESTIONS ARE GOOD

I adore young adults. I love their energy and capacity. I'm inspired by their spirit of inquiry and exploration as they negotiate the exhilarating though sometimes awkward transition into adulthood. Any chance to spend time with them is a bonus. So I was delighted to be called to teach an institute class for several years. I learned more from my students than they ever learned from me, but because of that assignment and several others, I know a *lot* of young men and women. And from time to time I get calls from those who want to talk about their boyfriends and girlfriends (or the lack thereof), their lives, their triumphs, and their worries.

Several years ago, a marvelous young woman who had just graduated with honors from BYU called me, distraught. Through sobs she blurted, "Sister Dew, I'm not sure I believe the Church is true, and I'm scared. What if my family isn't going to be together forever? What if what I've been taught my whole life isn't true?"

I listened to her attempt to explain her distress and finally asked, "Do you want to have a testimony?"

"Yes," she said.

"Are you willing to work for it?"

Again she answered, "Yes."

And was she ever! She had a superb bishop and ward Relief Society president, both of whom counseled repeatedly with her. Friends and family came to her rescue. She began to study the scriptures in a way she never had. And she and I began to meet for gospel study sessions. I told her, "Bring your scriptures, *Preach My Gospel*, and every question you have. Questions are good. Let's see what the Lord will teach us together."

She took me at my word and brought one thorny question after another. She asked question after question that I'd never considered—good, intelligent, probing questions. During one of our study sessions together, as she threw a steady stream of questions at me, I asked her if she was asking questions against a backdrop of faith or one of doubt. "In other words, are you saying, 'Here's something I don't understand, so the gospel must not be true,' or are you willing to say, 'Here's something I don't understand, but I wonder what the Lord or His prophets will teach us about this?' Are your questions asked with the assumption that there are answers? Are you willing to trust the Lord and give Him the benefit of the doubt?"

She was trying very hard to exercise faith, and so we pressed on. We searched the scriptures and the teachings of prophets for answers in session after session together. It was obvious to me that she *could* feel the presence and the confirming influence of the Spirit, but I wasn't sure if she recognized the source of her feelings. One day, as we read portions of a recent general conference address by a member of the Quorum of the Twelve, I could see that she was feeling something and asked what she thought her feelings meant. She acknowledged that she felt the Spirit as we read that talk.

"If you can feel the Spirit as we read the words of an Apostle, what does that mean?" I asked.

She finally responded, with a question in her voice, "That what he said must be true, because the Spirit wouldn't bear witness of something unless it was true? Right?"

Exactly.

Little by little, she began to realize that just because she had questions didn't mean she didn't have a testimony. The scriptures are filled with accounts of prophets who had questions. And my friend began to recognize when the Spirit was bearing witness to her—including bearing witness that prophets, seers, and revelators are truly prophets.

Her testimony slowly began to grow, our study sessions tapered off, and a couple of years passed. One Sunday evening she called to say: "I want you to be one of the first to know that I am holding in my hand a temple recommend. Will you come when I receive my endowment?" She added her thanks for the time we'd spent together and then said, "Do you know what you said that helped me the most? You told me to bring every question I had because questions are good. That simple statement allowed me to see myself as a seeker rather than as a doubter."

I hung up the phone and wiped away tears. What remarkable progress for that young woman!

Ironically, just two days later I received a much different call from another BYU graduate about the same age. "Sister Dew," she said, "before you hear it from someone else, I want you to know that I'm pregnant and, no, I haven't gotten married." She said that for several years she had doubted the truthfulness of the gospel and had finally decided that if she didn't believe in the Restoration, she didn't feel obligated to observe the Church's standards, including the law of chastity.

I told her that I was not her judge and that I loved her. Then I posed the same question I had asked the first girl: "Would you like to have a testimony?"

"No, I don't think so," she responded. "Not now."

I hung up the phone and wiped away tears from that phone call, too—but for a much different reason. The contrast was stunning. At about the same time, these two young women had encountered questions that threatened their testimonies. One of them had sent out a cry for help, and as a result, family, friends, and leaders had followed President Thomas S. Monson's counsel and gone to her rescue. The other girl had nursed her doubt and over time convinced herself that her immoral choices were acceptable. I believe in both of these girls and feel confident that the girl who thinks she doesn't want a testimony will at some point realize that she does. I'm certain it's there. But for now, she is walking a spiritually perilous path.

One girl's questions propelled her to become a seeker of truth. The other girl used her questions to justify choices that have had difficult consequences.

Questions are good. Questions are good *if* they are sincere questions, asked in faith, and asked of credible sources where the Spirit will direct and confirm the answers. Searching "*diligently* in the light of Christ" is the only way to "know good from evil" (Moroni 7:19; emphasis added). For "the Spirit speaketh the truth and lieth not. Wherefore, it speaketh of things as they really are, and of things as they really will be" (Jacob 4:13).

If we learn anything from the Prophet Joseph Smith, surely it is that the Father and the Son will respond to sincere questions, asked in faith. The Restoration was ushered in by the earnest question and sincere seeking of a fourteen-year-old. The Doctrine and Covenants is modern-day scripture filled with answers to the questions of that young Prophet. The magnificent revelation President Spencer W. Kimball received in June 1978 making it possible for all worthy males to be ordained to the priesthood came as a result of President Kimball's repeated pleadings with the

Lord over an extended period of time (see D&C Official Declaration 2). When President Thomas S. Monson announced in the October 2012 general conference that the age at which young men and women could be recommended for missionary service was being lowered to eighteen and nineteen, respectively, he acknowledged that the leaders of the Church had "prayerfully pondered" this matter.[1]

Asking inspired questions leads to knowledge. It leads to revelation. It leads to greater faith. And it leads to peace. Not asking questions, on the other hand, closes off revelation, growth, learning, progression, and the ministering of the Holy Ghost.

The scriptures are filled with warnings such as these:

"Wo unto the deaf that will not hear; for they shall perish. Wo unto the blind that will not see; for they shall perish also" (2 Nephi 9:31–32).

"He that will not hear my voice, the same shall ye not receive into my church" (Mosiah 26:28).

"Wo be unto him that hearkeneth unto the precepts of men, and denieth the power of God, and the gift of the Holy Ghost! Yea, wo be unto him that saith: We have received, and we need no more" (2 Nephi 28:26–27).

A pattern of not seeking help from heaven blocks revelation and leaves a person coping alone with downward spiraling thoughts or seeking out like-minded think-ers or even doubters in the blogosphere, in the theater, between the cov-ers of books—you name it. They can be found almost anywhere.

The Lord wants us to ask every probing question we can muster be-cause not asking questions can be far more dangerous than asking them. Alma taught that those who harden their hearts receive less and less until they "*know nothing* . . . ; and then they are taken captive by the devil, and led . . . down to destruction. Now this is what is meant by the chains of hell" (Alma 12:11; emphasis added). In other words, refusing to seek after truth makes you stupid. On the other hand, inspired questions asked in faith lead to truth—and "light and truth forsake that evil one" (D&C 93:37).

Nephi asked an inspired question in faith when he asked the Lord if he could see what his father saw. "After I had desired to know the things that my father had seen," Nephi recorded, "and believing that the Lord was able to make them known unto me, as I sat pondering in mine heart I was caught away in the Spirit of the Lord" (1 Nephi 11:1). What Nephi was then allowed to see far exceeded his request and no doubt his expectations as well.

The Lord responded by sending an angelic messenger to show Nephi the tree of life, the iron rod, the great and spacious building and mists of darkness, and the fruit of the tree, which is "sweet above all that is sweet" (Alma 32:42). The angel also explained the meaning of the vision along with the meanings of the images Nephi saw.

But the vision didn't stop there. Nephi saw the ministry of John the

Baptist and the Holy Ghost manifest in the form of a dove. He saw the birth, ministry, and Crucifixion of the Savior. He witnessed plain and precious truths being taken out of the Bible as well as the Apostles facing opposition after the Resurrection. He saw the Savior's visit to the Nephites and the wars that would rage between the posterity of Nephi and that of Laman and Lemuel. He saw two churches—the Church of the Lamb of God and the great and abominable church of the devil—and the havoc the latter wreaked. He saw the discovery of the promised land, the subsequent coming forth of latter-day scripture, the Restoration, and the building of Zion. And he saw the power the Saints in our day would possess to combat evil and persecution, and that we would be "armed with righteousness and with the power of God in great glory" (1 Nephi 14:14).

Nephi saw all this and much more, only to return to his father's tent to find Laman and Lemuel arguing about the meaning of their father's vision. When Nephi asked them, "Have ye inquired of the Lord?" they gave the classic response of doubters: "We have not; for the Lord maketh no such thing known unto us"—as though nothing were required of them (1 Nephi 15:8–9).

Nephi then attempted to teach his older brothers the pattern for receiving information through the Spirit: "Do ye not remember the things which the Lord hath said?" he asked. "If ye will not harden your hearts, and ask me in faith, believing that ye shall receive, with diligence in keeping my commandments, surely these things shall be made known unto you" (1 Nephi 15:11).

None of us are *entitled* to revelation without effort on our part. Answers from God don't just magically appear. If we want to grow spiritually, *the Lord expects us to ask questions and seek answers.* "If thou shalt ask," He promised, "thou shalt receive revelation upon revelation, knowledge upon knowledge, that thou mayest know the mysteries and peaceable things—that which bringeth joy, that which bringeth life eternal" (D&C 42:61). How much clearer can it be? The Lord loves inspired questions asked in humility and faith because they lead to knowledge, to revelation, and to greater faith.

The most effective leaders ask great questions, and they typically ask a lot of them. This is because the best leaders, regardless of the nature of their leadership, crave truth. They want to know what is real. They want to know how the members of their ward or branch really are, or what the children in their family really need, or how customers in their business really experience the service they receive. They aren't afraid of the answers to tough questions—including answers that may implicate them or spotlight their own weaknesses.

In like manner, the righteous also love truth. Whereas the "words of truth are hard against all uncleanness; . . . the righteous fear them not" (2 Nephi 9:40).

President Russell M. Nelson related an experience a stake president had in a stake council meeting as they wrestled with a difficult challenge: "At one point, [the stake president] realized that the stake Primary president had not spoken, so he asked if she had any impressions. 'Well, actually I have,' she said and then proceeded to share a thought that changed the entire direction of the meeting. The stake president continued, 'As she spoke, the Spirit testified to me that she had given voice to the revelation we had been seeking as a council.'"[2] That stake president was a leader who sought truth and was humble enough to acknowledge and accept it as it came through the process of counseling together.

The concept that information precedes inspiration is neither unique nor original, but it is important. Elder Neal A. Maxwell once said that he'd never met a man who was more inquisitive than President Gordon B. Hinckley. "If you sat next to him at dinner, he quizzed you all night," Elder Maxwell explained, adding that it didn't matter if President Hinckley was talking with a builder, a banker, or a security expert, he asked questions nonstop, always gathering information and learning. Similarly, after observing President Hinckley at a regional conference, then-Elder Russell M. Nelson reported: "One of the security officers assigned to us worked for the local police department. We had time between sessions, and President Hinckley grilled that officer for an hour about their procedures, techniques, and even the equipment they used. I marveled that he knew which questions to ask, each of which was law-enforcement specific."[3] And President Thomas S. Monson added: "President Hinckley [could] converse intelligently about anything with anyone. He [knew] how to ask the right questions. He [was] perfectly at home with high and low, and [could] converse with ease about everything from satellite technology to pruning trees."[4] His lifelong practice of asking questions not only helped him make connections with people everywhere but constantly added to his storehouse of knowledge and experience.

Questions are key to resolving conflict, to finding out what is really going on, to understanding the hearts and minds of others and engaging them in spirited discussion, to seeking answers through the Spirit, and to simply making fundamentally good decisions.

We all have questions, and we have them constantly. As human beings engaged in the mortal experience, we all encounter things that scare us, worry us, confuse us, hurt us, discourage us, puzzle us, and potentially threaten our faith and our progression.

Some of our questions are doctrinal, some are procedural or historical, and some are intensely personal. But we all have them.

Here are just some of the questions I've heard posed during the last few years. See if any of them strike a chord:

Why do I struggle to believe when no one else in my family does?

Should I go back to work and pursue a career?

If I get an advanced degree, will it limit the number of men who might be interested in me? Or will it send a signal to the Lord that I don't want to get married?

Should we have a baby?

Why can't we have a baby?

Whom should I marry?

Why have all of my friends married but I can't find anyone for me?

Why have some friends managed to get married more than once and I remain single?

Should I serve a mission?

Why did I serve a mission and not convert anyone?

Will the Lord forgive me for breaking my covenants?

Is there hope for me, after what I've done?

I came home early from my mission and now can't get over the feeling that I failed. What do I do now?

Is it all that serious to delay marriage a few years to finish my education and at least get a start on my career?

Is the prophet really a prophet? Does that mean he is infallible?

Did the Prophet Joseph Smith really have more than one wife? I've heard that some of his plural wives were young and others were already married to other men. How can that be right?

Why did my husband die so young?

Why did our child die when a priesthood blessing promised she would live?

How do I know if I'm receiving revelation?

Why can't we seem to get ahead financially even though we faithfully pay our tithing?Aren't the faithful supposed to prosper in the land?

Why have all of our children rejected the gospel? We tried so hard.

How can I stay sane and balance family, work, church duties, and LIFE and not buckle under the burden?

Given the increasing evil in the world, I long and pray for the Second Coming. There is a sternness in me about the wicked, and I struggle to love them. What would help me?

How do I continue to act with faith and choose hope?

My husband is on the journey of recovery from pornography addiction. I am trying to support him, but I feel like I need recovery myself. Where can I turn?

Do I dare get serious with a guy who has struggled with pornography?

Why don't the scriptures say much about women? Are women less important to the Lord than men?

Why aren't women eligible for priesthood ordination?

Why can't a woman stand in the circle when her baby is blessed?

How can I learn how the Atonement can help me?

What if the Church's position on gay marriage bothers me?

Why are the stipulations regarding baptism different for the children of gay parents than for the children of others who aren't actively participating in the Church?

Shouldn't my friends who are gay be able to have some happiness too?

Is it better to live life alone than to marry out of the faith?

Why can't I seem to conquer weaknesses that plague me?

How do I know if I am where the Lord wants me to be, doing what He wants me to do?

My parents divorced when I was a teenager, and there was contention in our home. I'm not sure I know how to make a marriage work. Where can I learn how?

How do I understand the temple when I can't even ask questions about it?

Will the Lord really help someone like me?

May I answer these questions, and *any* questions you may have, by posing a different question: *Are you willing to engage in the wrestle? In an ongoing spiritual wrestle?*

If we want to grow spiritually, the Lord expects us to ask questions and seek answers.

We live in a sound-bite world where "tweets," "likes," "posts," and "shares" have become the way we keep informed and share ideas. We are accustomed to expecting instant answers. But the most compelling questions in our lives rarely have quick, easy, Google answers. That is because receiving revelation and gaining knowledge, particularly divine knowledge, takes time.

It takes a wrestle.

CHAPTER 2

WRESTLING

The requirement to wrestle spiritually is not unique to our day. Enos described the "*wrestle* which [he] had before God, before [he] received a remission of [his] sins" (Enos 1:2; emphasis added). Alma described "*wrestling* with God in mighty prayer, that he would pour out his Spirit upon the people" of Ammonihah (Alma 8:10; emphasis added). Paul taught the Ephesians that "we *wrestle* not against flesh and blood, but against principalities, against powers, against the rulers of the darkness of this world, against spiritual wickedness in high places," and then he counseled them to put on the whole armor of God (Ephesians 6:12; emphasis added; see also v. 13).

Select any prophet, ancient or modern, and you'll find a lot of spiritual wrestling in both his life and his leadership. Imagine the pleadings of Joseph, who was sold into Egypt by his brothers; or Noah, as he and his family were confined to an ark without a clear understanding of what was to come. Imagine Brigham Young's supplications as he led a weary band of converts on a trek through an uncharted wilderness to a place he'd seen only in vision.

Wrestling is an interesting verb and an even more interesting sport. Champion wrestlers insist that it isn't necessarily the strongest wrestler or the one with the biggest muscle mass who wins. Winning wrestlers learn to leverage their strength to subdue, overpower, and defeat their opponents.

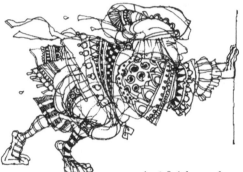

Spiritual wrestling leverages the strength of true doctrine to overpower our weaknesses, our wavering faith, and our lack of knowledge. Spiritual wrestlers are seekers. They are men and women of faith who want to understand more than they presently do and who are serious about increasing the light and knowledge in their lives. Brigham Young articulated the nature of this reality when he declared that "the men and women, who desire to obtain seats in the celestial kingdom, will find that they must battle every day."[5]

I have engaged in many a wrestle over the years, one of them recently. When the policy was announced that the children of gay parents might not be eligible for baptism at the traditional age of eight, I was confused. I did not question the Brethren or doubt their inspiration, but neither did

I understand the doctrinal basis for the policy. And my heart went out to friends with children or grandchildren in this situation. So I asked the Lord to teach me. I prayed, searched the scriptures, studied the teachings of prophets, and pondered this question in the temple. This went on for months. Then one day a colleague made a statement as part of a presentation that sparked a new thought for me, and in that moment the Spirit illuminated at least part of the doctrine in my heart and mind. I consider that answer personal revelation and not something I should repeat. Further, I am sure I still don't understand this issue in its entirety. So I continue to pray and ponder about it, seeking to learn more. But the spark of inspiration that day calmed me. Though I have wept with friends to whom this policy directly applies, understanding at least part of the related doctrine has given me a sense of peace.

When we have unresolved questions, our challenge does not lie in what we think we know. It lies in what we don't YET know.

Elder Neal A. Maxwell said it this way: "We should not assume . . . that just because something is unexplainable by us it is unexplainable."[6]

The Lord has promised to open the "eyes of our understandings" (D&C 76:19) and to "reveal all mysteries" (D&C 76:7). But He isn't likely to do either of these unless we seek to know. He will not force us to progress. Truman Madsen wrote of B. H. Roberts that "he could find nothing in the scriptures . . . to excuse anyone from brain sweat and from the arduous lifetime burden of seeking 'revelation upon revelation, knowledge upon knowledge.'"[7] In the same vein, Elder Richard G. Scott taught that "the Lord will not force you to learn. You must *exercise your agency* to authorize the Spirit to teach you." Elder Scott was describing an ongoing spiritual wrestle.[8]

No wonder the Lord wants us to ask every probing question we can muster. He wants us to exercise our agency to seek and learn, because in doing so we signal to the Lord what we truly care about.

Most spiritual growth, most revelation, most answers to difficult questions require us to wrestle spiritually. Remember my friend who thought she'd lost her testimony? Her doubt was triggered and subsequently fueled by a television drama featuring a scientist who didn't believe in God. I asked her, "You mean that a fictional character fabricated by a Hollywood writer who likely understands absolutely nothing about God has obliterated twenty-four years of gospel teaching?"

"But she's so smart," my friend replied.

There have always been and will always be charismatic men and women who can launch what *sound like*, on the surface, reasoned arguments against the Father and the Son, the Restoration, the Prophet Joseph Smith, the Book of Mormon, and living prophets. But doubters and pundits never tell the whole story, because they don't know the whole story—and typically don't want to know. They opt for clever sound bites, hoping no one digs deeper than they have.

Sound bites will never lead to a testimony. As seekers of truth, our safety lies in asking the right questions, in faith, and of the right sources—meaning those who *only* speak truth: the scriptures; prophets, seers, and revelators; and the Lord through the Holy Ghost.

President Spencer W. Kimball declared, "Why, oh, why do people think they can fathom the most complex spiritual depths without the necessary . . . *work* accompanied by compliance with the laws that govern it? Absurd it is, but you will . . . find popular personalities, who seem never to have lived a single law of God, discoursing . . . [about] religion. How ridiculous for such persons to attempt to outline for the world a way of life! . . . One cannot know God nor understand his works or plans unless he follows the laws which govern."[9]

Some answers and insights come from prophets, seers, and revelators as well as other faithful and earnest seekers of light and truth. But spiritual work is just that—work. The answers don't always come quickly. Revelation tends to come line upon line, and sometimes syllable upon syllable. We have no doubt all wished for revelation that would come, even once in a while, paragraph upon paragraph. But typically, receiving revelation is rigorous spiritual work.

My life has been filled with spiritual wrestling—not because of any great valor on my part but because I have yearned to understand why certain things were happening to me, and why others were not. For decades I have fasted, prayed, and pleaded for a husband. I've asked who he is, where he is, and when he's coming. As of this writing, I still don't know the answer to any of those questions. But the wrestle has blessed me with the knowledge that Jesus Christ is *my* Savior, that His gospel is filled with power, and that God will talk to and direct me.

The wrestle is never easy, and it does not always lead to the answers or results we desire. But there is always a reward of some kind—whether that reward comes in the form of knowledge and revelation, greater faith, or more peace.

Some time ago, I was invited to deliver the keynote address at the BYU Women's Conference. The theme of that conference was the grace of the Lord Jesus Christ, and I felt overwhelmed by the assignment. I knew I did not understand grace well enough to teach it in a way that the Spirit could endorse the message.

So I went to work. I fasted and prayed, pored over the scriptures, went to the temple, and pleaded for spiritual enlightenment. I was essentially asking for the grace, or power, of the Lord to help me understand the grace of the Lord. It was a grueling process, particularly as the conference neared and I had volumes of notes but no talk.

But then, little by little, the Spirit began to not only clarify points of doctrine but bring to my mind experiences I'd had throughout my life that were clearly manifestations of grace—though I had not always realized it at the time. In the grace of the Lord, I saw more clearly than I ever had how frequently He had been lifting and carrying and healing me. Ultimately, the wrestling involved in creating that talk blessed me more, I'm sure, than anyone who heard that message. When we are willing to wrestle spiritually, we're in a better position to help others—but we are always the ones who benefit most.

That point was illustrated in dramatic fashion through an experience I had while serving as a member of the Relief Society general presidency. One of the privileges general officers of the Church have is the chance, from time to time, to be taught by prophets, seers, and revelators. One such opportunity occurred semiannually in connection with general conference, when general officers were invited to attend sessions of General Authority training.

Those experiences were always inspiring and informative, and I never took for granted the opportunities to learn from our leaders. But one training session had a very pronounced effect on me personally.

That particular four-hour session was designed to help General Authorities and general officers discuss how to better help strengthen the families of the Church. The senior General Authority conducting the session posed many questions of those in attendance and invited an open exchange of ideas and impressions.

But from the outset, this General Authority did something unusual in the way he accepted comments from the General Authorities and general officers in attendance. Whenever someone responded to a question and used the word woman to describe a female's participation in the family, the conducting officer corrected that person and told him or her to use the word mother instead. The same held true for references to men, who were to be referred to only as fathers.

At first I didn't think much of it, but as the morning wore on, and as the point was repeatedly made that women were mothers and men were fathers, I began to shrink in my chair. By the end of the morning, I felt branded. I was painfully aware of the fact that I was the only person in the room who had never married, the only one who was not a mother or father. And though there likely wasn't another person present who gave it a second thought, I felt—for the first time in my Church life—like an outsider who did not belong.

When the session ended, I got out of that room as quickly as I could and hurried back to my office in the Relief Society Building, where I closed the door and cried. I had wrestled for years to deal with my marital status, but I had never felt that I didn't have a place in the Church. Prior to my then-current service in a general presidency, I had served as a stake Relief Society president and as a counselor in a stake auxiliary presidency, as a ward Relief Society president and as a counselor, and as a member of the Relief Society general board. I had never felt left out or excluded. Until that morning. And, to make matters worse, I felt excluded by prophets, seers, and revelators, which *in that moment* made me wonder how the Lord really felt about me. It was painful.

I'm sorry to say that I responded by stewing about what had happened. At first, I was just hurt. But then I became angry. "How can they disenfranchise an entire segment of Church members?" I asked myself. And I stewed some more.

There I was, a general officer who felt wounded by a General

Authority. Who could I talk to? I couldn't quite picture going to my bishop and telling him I was upset with an Apostle. So, I did the next worst thing. I continued to stew.

This went on for several months, until the time came for me to begin working on the address I was to give at the upcoming general Relief Society meeting. I prayed, pondered, fasted, went to the temple again and again, and . . . nothing. I had absolutely no ideas, no inspiration, nothing. The heavens were sealed. This went on for several weeks, and as the calendar raced by, I began to panic. I increased my praying, fasting, and worshipping in the temple.

Finally I received one clear impression: that I needed to resolve my feelings about that General Authority. The impression came as a gentle reprimand, and I knew it was true. I *did* need to resolve my feelings—which included repenting for having them. Finally, with some humility imposed by the crisis I was in regarding that talk, I got on my knees and asked for forgiveness. Then I asked two questions I should have posed several months earlier, questions that could have spared me a lot of anguish: *Was there something I missed in that meeting? Did I misunderstand the intent of that General Authority?*

A day or two later I had another clear impression—that I should speak in the general Relief Society meeting about, of all things, motherhood.

"You've got to be kidding," I thought. But the impression was clear, so I began to search the scriptures and the teachings of prophets. I went to the temple again and again, paid closer attention to the account depicted in the endowment, and pondered what a friend of mine, by then deceased, might have meant when he referred to the endowment as "Eve's show." And I prayed and prayed. In other words, in a spirit of humility—finally—I wrestled. I wrestled to understand the doctrine of motherhood, and I wrestled with my own feelings about that doctrine.

And guess what I learned? That General Authority had been exactly right. I learned that every woman is a mother! Regardless of her life circumstances, each woman has been divinely endowed with the gift of motherhood—with the gift of bearing, and bearing with, the children of God in the sacred process of helping nurture them along the path that leads to exaltation.

Engaging in this wrestle led to an address entitled "Are We Not All Mothers?" that attempted to articulate the doctrine of motherhood. In the process, for the first time in my life, I felt peace about not having had the privilege of bearing children here on this earth. It was as the Lord told Joseph Smith and Oliver Cowdery, "Did I not speak peace to your mind concerning the matter? What greater witness can you have than from God?" (D&C 6:23). This is not to say that the longing for a family of my own went away. It didn't and it hasn't. But the deep, latent pain I had tried to suppress for years was gone. In response to repentance and earnest wrestling, the Savior healed that pain while teaching me a profoundly crucial doctrine.

I don't have the answers to every question I've asked or pondered. There are plenty of questions and issues I have not resolved. But as I've been willing to wrestle, sometimes for years at a time, the Lord has taught me. I've received enough enlightenment enough times to know that there is always more to learn, always greater light and knowledge available. When we are willing to wrestle spiritually for knowledge and revelation, the Spirit will enlighten us, guide us to truth, and bless us with peace of heart and mind.

The Lord needs men and women who can talk with confidence about what they believe. Men and women who aren't afraid to wrestle with tough questions. Men and women who can talk to children, youth, and each other about everything from the Church's teachings about marriage to other issues that can cause confusion and threaten faith.

We of all people should be comfortable discussing any topic, any issue, any doctrine with anyone, because we can draw from a deep reservoir of revealed truth. We have so many places to turn for answers—to the Lord, to the scriptures, to prophets, seers, and revelators, and to a host of other inspired resources.[10]

The Lord needs men and women who know how to get answers. Men and women who aren't easily deceived and whose testimonies aren't shaken by someone with carefully crafted talking points. Men and women whose faith isn't threatened when they don't have all the answers and can't always effectively respond to alternate points of view. Men and women who have had witness after witness that Jesus is the Christ and that His gospel has been restored—so that when circumstances confuse or discourage them, they turn toward the Savior rather than away from Him. And men and women who are secure enough in their own testimonies that they can help others who are struggling to find their way.

He needs men and women who are willing to engage in the wrestle.

CHAPTER 3

RECEIVING ANSWERS

In August 1970, a worldwide Laurel Leadership Conference was held at BYU, with some 2,500 Laurel-age girls participating. I was one of those girls, and for a Midwest farmer's daughter who had just bounced off a turnip truck, it was a remarkable experience. I had previously visited BYU, so the surroundings were familiar. But I had never seen so many LDS girls my age. It was overwhelming to walk into the Wilkinson Center ballroom and find it filled with Laurels.

This many years later, I don't remember many specifics about that conference. But there was one meeting I'll never forget. It was the sacrament meeting held on Sunday with President Harold B. Lee, then First Counselor in the First Presidency, presiding.

I remember how I felt when we all stood as President Lee entered that large ballroom. And I remember two things he said when he addressed us: first, that if our testimonies were weak, we could lean on his until ours grew stronger; and second, that if we wanted to, we could have a spiritual experience every day. In fact, he encouraged us to *seek* to have a spiritual experience every day. He did not, as I recall, promise we would have one every day, but counseled us to seek experiences with the Spirit daily.

President Lee's second point resonated with me. I couldn't imagine that such a thing was possible. I had felt the presence of the Spirit many times. But to have a spiritual experience—whatever that meant—regularly? It seemed impossible to this high-school senior. However, I believed what a prophet, seer, and revelator promised us.

Throughout the more than four decades that have transpired since that memorable sacrament meeting, I have thought often about President Lee's wisdom in suggesting such an aspiration for a group of young women who would soon become wives, mothers, leaders, and teachers in the Church. Those who seek regularly for revelation, knowledge, and witnesses of the Spirit are simply better positioned to deal with life's questions, disappointments, and perplexities.

What President Lee promised a group of seniors in high school is true for all of us. If we seek to have regular experiences with the Spirit, we will have them. It takes spiritual work, and usually it takes wrestling—an ongoing spiritual wrestle that becomes a regular part of life rather than something engaged in only when trouble hits. But the Lord is eager to communicate with us through the manifestations and promptings of the Holy Ghost. And the cumulative effect of repeated witnesses of the Spirit becomes something of an inoculation against the ups and downs, the confusion and bewilderment, and the plain old agonies of life. When we put ourselves in a position to feel the Spirit and receive repeated confirmations from heaven, we also put ourselves in a position to counteract deception, distortion, and untruths.

The Prophet Joseph spoke frequently about seeking truth from the purest of sources: "I have an old edition of the New Testament in the Latin, Hebrew, German and Greek languages. . . . I thank God that I have got this old book; but I thank him more for the gift of the Holy Ghost. . . . The Holy Ghost . . . comprehends more than all the world; and I will associate myself with him."[11]

The Prophet Joseph also taught that we must all "grow into the principle of revelation."[12] And then, in a frequently quoted but astonishing statement, he tried to enlarge our vision about the revelation available to each of us: "God hath not revealed anything to Joseph, but what He will make known unto the Twelve, and even the least Saint may know all things as fast as he is able to bear them, for the day must come when no man need say to his neighbor, Know ye the Lord; for all shall know Him . . . from the least to the greatest."[13] The Apostle Paul taught the same thing: "Ye may all prophesy. . . . *Covet to prophesy*" (1 Corinthians 14:31, 39;

35

emphasis added). Every member of the Church can and should be seeking to receive revelation for his or her own life.

President Henry B. Eyring put a fine point on how vital it is that we learn to receive revelation: "We all know that human judgment and logical thinking will not be enough to get *answers to the questions* that matter most in life. We need revelation from God. And we will need not just one revelation in a time of stress, but we need a constantly renewed stream. We need not just one flash of light and comfort, but we need the continuing blessing of communication with God."[14]

Growing spiritually and receiving answers to our questions depends upon our ability to *feel, hear,* and *understand* the whisperings of the Spirit. It is worth engaging in a spiritual wrestle to learn to receive personal revelation, because we can know what is true only when the Spirit bears witness to both our hearts and minds in the way only the Holy Ghost can.

The Lord in essence defined revelation when He told Joseph Smith and Oliver Cowdery, "I will tell you in your mind and in your heart, by the Holy Ghost, which shall come upon you and which shall dwell in your heart. Now, behold, this is the spirit of revelation" (D&C 8:2–3). Or, said another way, we are to "seek learning, even by study and also by faith" (D&C 88:118).

Learning and receiving revelation must necessarily include both the heart and the mind, or thoughts and feelings. Intellect alone cannot produce a testimony. You cannot *think* your way to conversion, because *you cannot convince your mind of something your heart does not feel.*

Learning by study—wrestling to gain knowledge—is crucial not only to gaining and strengthening your testimony but to answering the most challenging questions of your life. Remember the young adult woman who thought she didn't have a testimony but who, in a sheer act of faith, answered "yes" when I asked if she was willing to work for one? She immersed herself in the scriptures more intently than ever before, studied and pondered the teachings of prophets, seers, and revelators, and turned to other inspired sources as well.

She did what Elder Richard G. Scott counseled when he taught that "to gain knowledge of great worth requires extraordinary personal effort. This is particularly true when our desire is to obtain spiritual knowledge."[10] In sharp contrast to this, Nephi lamented that he mourned because of the "ignorance" of his people, who would "not search knowledge, nor understand great knowledge, when it is given unto them in plainness, even as plain as word can be" (2 Nephi 32:7).

Thus, learning and receiving revelation depend upon our increasing our knowledge of the doctrine of the gospel of Jesus Christ. But intellect and reason must be combined with the impressions of the Spirit upon our hearts, because the heart is the ultimate instrument of conversion.

Abinadi told the wicked priests of King Noah that they had not applied their "hearts to understanding" (Mosiah 12:27; see also 13:11). King Benjamin prefaced his address to his people by counseling them to open their "hearts that ye may understand" (Mosiah 2:9). When the multitude gathered to hear the Savior at the Temple Mount in Bountiful, the people's "hearts were open and they did understand" (3 Nephi 19:33). In Proverbs, we are admonished to apply our "heart to understanding" (Proverbs 2:2). And Alma made it clear that "he that will harden his heart, the same receiveth the lesser portion of the word; and he that will not harden his heart, to him is given the greater portion of the word, until it is given unto him to know the mysteries of God until he know them in full" (Alma 12:10).

Intellect is important. The ability and willingness to ponder, think, and reason through issues is crucial. But intellect alone will not lead to conversion, because *true conversion happens in the heart.*

No wonder that throughout scripture there is such emphasis on the heart—a change of heart, a soft heart, an open heart, a new heart. When someone says, "My mind is made up," it usually means that the person's heart is closed to considering other ideas. When the heart is not open, there are limits to the influence the Spirit can have. A penetrating spiritual witness is unlikely to occur in someone whose heart is closed. On the other hand, people who are seeking revelation have open hearts, meaning they are open to new ideas, to impressions they haven't had before, and to revelation.

Elder Jeffrey R. Holland taught that "revelation almost always comes in response to a question, usually an urgent question—not always but usually. In that sense it does provide information, but it is urgently needed information. . . . Moses' challenge was how to get himself and the children of Israel out of [the] horrible predicament they were in. There were chariots behind them, sand dunes on every side, and just a lot of water immediately ahead. He needed information all right—what to do—but it wasn't a casual thing he was asking. In this case it was literally a matter of life and death. You will need information, too, but in matters of great consequence it is not likely to come unless you want it urgently, faithfully, humbly. Moroni calls it seeking 'with real intent.' (Moroni 10:4). If you can seek that way, and stay in that mode, not much that the adversary can counter with will dissuade you from a righteous path."[16]

In my early twenties, I admitted to a friend and mentor that I could feel the presence of the Spirit but couldn't discern specific answers. He asked me if I had asked the Lord to teach me His language—meaning, what it felt and sounded like when He was speaking *to me*. I hadn't, but that night I began to ask the Lord to teach me the language of revelation.

Among other things, through the years it has become apparent that seekers have certain habits that are key to learning to communicate with God. For starters, they engage in the wrestle, meaning they work at it. They immerse themselves regularly in the scriptures, which are the textbook for the Lord's language. And seekers listen. One of my former institute students periodically turns everything electronic off. TV off. Music off. Phone off. Computer and iPad off. She says, "I like to let the Lord know I'm listening."

Seekers also work to be increasingly pure—pure in their heart, thoughts, and motives; pure in what they say, watch, read, and listen to; even pure in what they wear—meaning avoiding suggestive or provocative attire. Purity invites the Spirit, and it increases light. And "he that receiveth light, and continueth in God, receiveth more light; and that light growth brighter and brighter until the perfect day" (D&C 50:24). Light is a powerful antidote to anything evil because darkness cannot persist in the presence of light.[17]

Our own sins can keep us from receiving the light we seek. Even seemingly small transgressions can be dangerous. As C. S. Lewis said, "It does not matter how small the sins are, provided that their cumulative effect is to edge the man away from the Light and out into the Nothing. Murder is no better than cards if cards can do the trick."[18]

I have lived alone for most of my adult life, and I don't recommend it. BYU President Kevin J Worthen stated that "no one can flourish in isolation,"[19] and I can vouch for that! I learned long ago that to hold loneliness at bay, I had to create an environment at home where the Spirit and angels would be willing to come. Elder Jeffrey R. Holland counseled us to "cultivate and be where the Spirit of the Lord is. Make sure that includes your home."[20] His counsel has been a lifeline for me.

As you create a spiritual environment at home, cultivate spiritual habits, and seek to recognize the Lord's hand in your life, there are two questions that will help open the heavens. First, ask the Lord to teach you what it feels and sounds like *for you* when He is speaking to you via the Holy Ghost. Then watch how He tutors you—including the scriptures you're drawn to, the emphases in general conference messages you may have missed the first time around, and so on.

Second, if you've never asked the Lord how He feels about you, that is a great question to ask. Over time, He will tell you, and, as He does, you'll learn more about discerning revelation through the Spirit.

Cultivating the capacity to feel the presence and hear the whisperings of the Spirit is central to living a life based *intentionally* upon the Spirit. When the Lord sees that we want to communicate with Him, He will teach us how. Imagine what would happen if we were as intent on trying to connect with heaven as we are with monitoring everyone's latest post on our social media feeds. Imagine what could happen if those people who search for things to criticize in the Church were to apply the same energy to learning how God works.

We live in a time when the keys of the Melchizedek Priesthood are upon the earth. That priesthood holds the "keys of all the spiritual blessings of the church"—including "the privilege of receiving the mysteries of the kingdom of heaven," of having "the heavens opened" to us, of communing "with the general assembly and church of the Firstborn," and of enjoying "the communion and presence of God the Father, and Jesus the mediator of the new covenant" (D&C 107:18–19). We live in the one dispensation in the history of the earth during which "nothing shall be withheld" (D&C 121:28).

There were things the Savior did not and could not teach His own people in the meridian of time. There were things the Nephites did not know. But the only limitations on us are those we place upon ourselves through our disobedience or failure to seek, our laziness or apathy.

The Lord told Joseph Smith there were sweeping spiritual privileges available for those living in our dispensation, describing them with this imagery: "As well might man stretch forth his puny arm to stop the Missouri river in its decreed course, or to turn it up stream, as to hinder the Almighty from pouring down knowledge from heaven upon the heads of the Latter-day Saints" (D&C 121:33). Imagine the implications! *No spiritual privileges are withheld* today from the faithful who seek them repeatedly and diligently.

Learning how to pierce the veil and gain the help of heaven, how to have greater access to the power of God and the sweeping array of spiritual privileges available to us, and how to receive revelation requires us to learn what the gospel of Jesus Christ actually entails. It means learning the "peaceable things of the kingdom" (D&C 36:2), which tend to be truths we won't find in a Sunday School manual but are doctrinal insights that come largely through the tutoring of the Spirit.

Nephi admonishes us to feast upon the words of Christ, and he warns that if we cannot receive revelation, it is "because [we] ask not, neither do [we] knock; wherefore, [we] are not brought into the light, but must perish in the dark." Nephi then laments that far too many will "not search knowledge, nor understand great knowledge, when it is given unto [us] in plainness, even as plain as word can be" (2 Nephi 32:4, 7).

Nephi's brother Jacob no doubt learned from his older brother the kinds of spiritual privileges available to the faithful. In his youth he beheld the Savior's glory (see 2 Nephi 2:4). He saw the Savior's Crucifixion (see 2 Nephi 6:9). He had the faith to work miracles. If we knew nothing else about Jacob, the following statement would tell us everything we need to know: "Wherefore, we search the prophets, and we have many revelations and the spirit of prophecy; and having all these witnesses we obtain a hope, and our faith becometh unshaken, insomuch that we truly can command in the name of Jesus and the very trees obey us, or the mountains, or the waves of the sea" (Jacob 4:6).

Searching the prophets suggests *more* than reading or even studying. It implies spiritually wrestling. When we are willing to work, the Lord will teach us, open our eyes to things we haven't seen before, and lead us along as we grow in our understanding about the truths of the gospel.

There is, of course, a fundamental challenge: *We are imperfect people trying to understand and communicate a perfect message.* Therein lies the source of many challenges. As one example, being offended by how others fulfill their callings or express their feelings about the gospel is a fruitless exercise. We are all mortals, and we all make mistakes, offend each other, "undersell" or misrepresent truths, and at times even teach (usually unknowingly) false doctrine. Imagine how much false doctrine is taught around the world on any given Sunday simply because the Lord has entrusted that teaching to millions of imperfect people whose knowledge and ability to impart that knowledge are insufficient (meaning, all of us). He is apparently not terribly worried about that, though. The greater concern is when we stop seeking to understand how much the Lord will make available to those who love and follow Him.

Recently, a friend working on her PhD received an impression during a Relief Society conference to shift the focus of her dissertation. She also felt prompted to go directly to the temple following the meeting to ask the Lord further questions. She said, "While there, I was told how to make [this new focus] work, . . . [and] how I could be both academically unbiased and spiritually honest. I occasionally receive clear words from the

Spirit, but never have I been given such clear instructions. . . . The task ahead feels incredibly difficult, but I know what direction to go and that the Lord expects it of me, and that makes all the difference."[21]

Receiving revelation is key to receiving answers to our questions. Revelation may not come quickly, easily, or clearly. And the Lord may choose to answer a different question from the one you've asked. But revelation *always* comes.

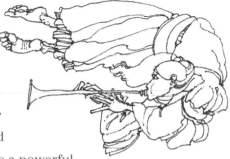

One of the profound privileges of membership in The Church of Jesus Christ of Latter-day Saints is that none of us have to take anyone else's word for what is true. Personal revelation is a powerful, persuasive antidote to uncertainty and confusion.

Those who have the Holy Ghost and who diligently seek will find. Period. "For he that diligently seeketh shall find; and the mysteries of God shall be unfolded unto them, by the power of the Holy Ghost" (1 Nephi 10:19).

Receiving revelation is one of the most delicious fruits of engaging in an ongoing spiritual wrestle.

CHAPTER 4

WALKING BY FAITH

Men and women of faith are required to have faith. Yet learning to walk by faith is surely one of the most difficult transitions we make as mortals. Our natural tendency is to want answers. We like things tied up neatly with a bow—although almost nothing ever is. We don't like or always know how to respond to ambiguity. The simple but agonizing fact is that followers of Jesus Christ are required to walk by faith, to at least some degree, and there is nothing easy about it.

Gratefully, we are not left alone in the quest to increase our faith. The Lord told Joseph Smith that one reason the Church was restored was so that "faith also might increase in the earth" (D&C 1:21), and that those who served Him "in righteousness and in truth" would be eligible to learn "all mysteries, yea, all the hidden mysteries of my kingdom from days of old, and for ages to come. . . . Yea, even the wonders of eternity shall they know" (D&C 76:5, 7–8).

The very process of wrestling with sincere questions, and learning more and more about how God works, is fundamental to building and increasing our faith. Although the Lord will reveal many things to us, *He has never told His covenant people everything about everything.* We are admonished to "doubt not, but be believing" (Mormon 9:27).

*But "doubting not" does not mean understanding everything—*including His timing. It means not doubting that God knows more than we do—that "all things have been [and are] done in the wisdom of him who knoweth all things" (2 Nephi 2:24). It means, as King Benjamin admonished his people, believing that God is, "that he created all things, both in heaven and in earth; [believing] that he has all wisdom, and all power, both in heaven and in earth; [believing] that man doth not comprehend all the things which the Lord can comprehend" (Mosiah 4:9). It also means understanding that there will be challenges to the Lord's people and to His Church. President Gordon B. Hinckley was clear about this: "The Lord never said that there would not be troubles. Our people have known afflictions of every sort as those

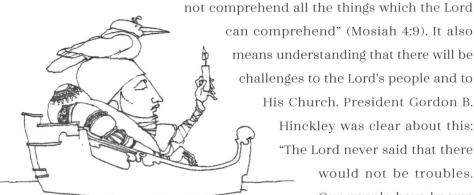

who have opposed this work have come upon them. But faith has shown through all their sorrows. This work has consistently moved forward and has never taken a backward step since its inception. . . . Whether we as individuals go forward will depend on us. But the Church will never fail to move forward."[22]

Thus, doubting is not synonymous with the pursuit of truth, nor is it the same as asking questions. To doubt is to reject truth and faith. Further, there is a spirit of doubt that the adversary uses very effectively. It has more to do with temptation than it does with a lack of faith, though it can look and feel as though it is the latter. At its most fundamental level, doubting means doubting the Father and His Son. As covenant sons and daughters—as people of faith—we are required to have faith, to live by faith, to "ask in faith, nothing wavering" (James 1:6), and to "overcome by faith" (D&C 76:53). These repeated admonitions to build our faith are crucial because it is much easier to sow doubt than to build faith and to learn by faith. When all is said and done, learning by faith is as crucial as learning by study, because there are some things we cannot learn from a book.

Elder Dallin H. Oaks underscored this truth: "After all we can publish, our members are sometimes left with basic questions that cannot be resolved by study. . . . Some things can be learned only by faith. Our ultimate reliance must be on faith in the witness we have received from the Holy Ghost."[23]

President Harold B. Lee said something similar: "It is not the function of religion to answer all the questions about God's moral government of the universe, but to give one courage, through faith, to go on in the face of questions he never finds the answer to in his present status."[24]

And in an address to Church Educational System administrators and teachers, Elder Jeffrey R. Holland delivered this stirring declaration about the relationship of questions to revealed truth: "Not all gospel questions have answers—yet—but they will come. In the meantime, I have a question. What conceivable historical or doctrinal or procedural issue that may arise among any group could ever overshadow or negate one's consuming spiritual conviction regarding the Father's merciful plan of salvation; His Only Begotten Son's birth, mission, Atonement, and Resurrection; the reality of the First Vision; the restoration of the priesthood; the receipt of divine revelation, both personally and institutionally; the soul-shaping spirit and moving power of the Book of Mormon; the awe and majesty of the temple endowment; one's own personal experience with true miracles; and on and on and on? Talk about a question! It is a mystery to me how those majestic, eternal, first-level truths so central to the grandeur of the *whole* gospel message can be set aside or completely dismissed by some in favor of obsessing over second- or third- or fourth-level pieces of that whole. To me, this is, in words attributed to Edith Wharton, truly being trapped in 'the thick of thin things.'"[25]

All questions have answers. But some questions, be they personal, doctrinal, or procedural, may not be answered until later. Some may not be answered in this life. Some ambiguity about the way God works with His children and in the governance of His Church may always exist. And certainly, some ironies, the likes of which we find frequently in scripture—such as "the first shall be last" and "lose your life to find it"—may always typify our lives here.

Hence the ongoing need to strengthen and increase our faith, because faith does not stand still. It is either increasing or disappearing. As President Henry B. Eyring has said, "Faith has a short shelf life."[26]

Consider the verse that sent Joseph to the grove: "If any of you lack wisdom, let him ask of God, that giveth to all men liberally, and upbraideth not; and it shall be given him." James then added this stipulation: "But let him ask in faith, *nothing wavering*" (James 1:5–6; emphasis added).

Thus, once the Spirit has borne witness to you of truth, particularly the foundational truths that comprise a testimony—that God is our Father, that Jesus is the Christ, that Joseph Smith was the prophet called to restore the Savior's gospel, that the Book of Mormon is scripture, and that we are led by prophets, seers, and revelators today—then you *know* the gospel is true. You have a testimony! And even though you do not know or understand all things, you can feel secure in what you *do* know!

If Joseph Smith was a prophet called to restore the Savior's Church, and if the Book of Mormon is the word of God, and if prophets lead us today, then the Church is true.

At that point, when questions arise or when blessings you've been pleading for remain unfulfilled, these issues are not an indication that you don't have a testimony or that the gospel is not true. They are an invitation for you to grow spiritually.

Sometimes we become confused about the intersection of questions and testimony and attempt to connect them when they are not necessarily related. Questions should never threaten a testimony; they should only help build conviction, deepen understanding, and increase faith—because they provide the opportunity to learn.

Admittedly, it can sometimes feel as though our questions about doctrine or Church procedures or the Church's history or unfulfilled personal blessings are somehow connected to our testimonies. If you have been pleading for healing or marriage or a child without a fulfillment of those pleadings, it can be tempting to wonder if God is real, if He's listening, or if He cares. And if Church doctrine on a particular issue conflicts with your personal views, it can feel confusing. If certain procedures or practices in the Church puzzle you, it can feel discouraging. Any of those emotions or sensations, left in isolation, can threaten testimony.

But I repeat: Once you have received a spiritual witness of the truths that form the foundation of a testimony, then when questions arise—even the thorniest questions about our doctrine or history or positions on sensitive issues, or the aching desires of our hearts—they are opportunities for personal, spiritual growth. They are not red flags suggesting that the gospel isn't true. They are opportunities to engage in the wrestle for inspired answers, receive personal revelation, and increase faith.

I have plenty of unanswered questions. Some are doctrinal. Some concern procedural or other aspects of the Church. And some are intensely, agonizingly personal. But those questions have nothing to do with my absolute conviction that the Savior's Church has been restored and that The Church of Jesus Christ of Latter-day Saints is it.

I began to understand this distinction years ago when a deep personal disappointment left me depressed and angry with the Lord. In an effort to find some peace, I wrestled with feelings of hurt and pain and rejection. I still remember the moment when I realized that for someone who has a testimony—and I did—there is no choice but to go forward with faith, trusting the Lord to open doors of understanding and healing. Now, three decades later, the Spirit has borne witness to me so many times of so many things that to question the veracity of the Church simply because I have unanswered questions or unanswered prayers would cut off the very source of future revelation, healing, and peace.

Instead, questions, *especially* the tough ones, propel us to engage in a spiritual wrestle so that the Lord can lead us along. Without plain old spiritual work, even God can't make us grow—or at least, He won't.

Sometimes the Lord doesn't answer our questions or pleadings right away because we're not ready for the answer. "Ye cannot bear all things now," He once told Joseph Smith, but then added these words of comfort: "Nevertheless, be of good cheer, for I will lead you along" (D&C 78:18).

Some of the best people who have ever lived have been required to exercise faith as the Lord leads them along. Imagine the questions Noah must have had, not to mention Noah's wife, as they boarded an ark filled with smelly animals. We know something of Nephi's agony as he stood over a drunken Laban, wondering if he had the faith to slay a man as commanded by the Lord (see 1 Nephi 4:10–11).

David showed astonishing faith when he confronted the giant Goliath. Choosing to use a slingshot and five smooth stones rather than heavy armor and a sword, he appealed to heaven for help and believed the Lord would help him: "The Lord that delivered me out of the paw of the lion, and out of the paw of the bear, he will deliver me out of the hand of this Philistine" (1 Samuel 17:37).

The Lord instructed Nephi to build a ship "after the manner which I shall show thee," which was "not after the manner of men," and Nephi had the faith to receive the Lord's instruction and follow through on it (1 Nephi 17:8; 18:2).

As challenging as it can be to build and live by faith, doing so makes it possible to do more and accomplish more than we ever could on our own.

Elder Ezra Taft Benson exemplified this truth when, in December 1946, with World War II finally over, President George Albert Smith called him to serve as president of the European Mission. The call meant going to Europe for an undetermined amount of time to reestablish contact with the Saints who had survived the brutality of war and to distribute much-needed welfare supplies.

What Elder Benson found in Europe defied description. There were no phones, no roads, no cars for civilians, no reliable transportation, little food, and very little communication of any kind. In most places he was the first foreign civilian to travel through the occupied areas of Germany, Czechoslovakia, and Poland. Repeatedly he was told that he couldn't get a car, but then he would find a car. He was refused seats on the few planes flying, but somehow he managed to secure seats on planes. He was forbidden from proceeding beyond certain points, but then he would persuade a military officer to allow him to proceed. He sometimes went days without eating and often slept on smelly straw ticks on floors. Day after day, he prayed and pleaded with heaven and then went to work. Sometimes his wrestle was with government bureaucracy and military leaders. Sometimes it was to receive revelation. Sometimes it was to overcome his own uncertainty. But he pressed on, trusting the Lord to open necessary doors.

As one example, in Frankfurt, Elder Benson needed permission from General Joseph T. McNarney to go deeper into the occupied areas of Germany. The general's aide said it would take at least three days to arrange for an appointment. Elder Benson went back to the car, prayed, and then returned immediately to the general's office, only to find a different aide there who ushered Elder Benson in to meet with the general.

General McNarney was initially annoyed by this American making the absurd request to travel throughout war-torn Germany, Austria, and Czechoslovakia. But Elder Benson talked to him until a softening came over the man. Finally he said, "Mr. Benson, there's something about you that I like. I want to help you." When Elder Benson explained that the Church had warehouses full of food and clothing that could be shipped immediately, the general was amazed: "Mr. Benson, I have never heard of a church with such vision."

McNarney warned that they would be the first American civilians to travel to Berlin by car and that the military could take no responsibility for their safety, but he authorized them to proceed.

What Elder Benson found in Berlin was beyond description. "I witnessed scenes that seemed almost outside this world," he recorded. "I smelled the odor of decaying, human bodies. . . . I saw old men and women with small hatchets eagerly digging at tree stumps and roots in an effort to get scraps of fuel. . . . Later I faced in a cold, half-wrecked auditorium off a bombed street 480 cold, half-starved but faithful Latter-day Saints. . . . Yet there was no bitterness or anger but a sweet . . . expression of faith in the gospel."

An experience in Oslo was indicative of countless others. A heavy snowstorm canceled his plane back to London, but he needed desperately to return in order to meet other commitments. Local Church leaders urged him to spend the night at their home, but he insisted on staying at the airport. Finally, the weather cleared enough for one plane to take off. As cargo was loaded onto the plane, and then as the plane taxied away from the terminal, Elder Benson stood watching. The plane went out to the runway and paused for several minutes. Then, without warning, it taxied back, and a man got off and ran into the terminal. "Where is that man who says he must get to London tonight? If he'll sit in the cargo hold with the mail bags, he can come." It was a frigid flight, but Elder Benson returned to London.

In a letter to the First Presidency, Elder Benson summarized the challenge: "The job of taking care of our Saints even as to their most meager needs is overwhelming, and as we contemplate their rehabilitation it becomes staggering." But then he added, "The Lord is blessing our efforts, and I am sure He will continue to do so if we do our best."

Day after day, for eleven months, he prayed and pleaded and worked and wrestled. And he went forward every day with faith that the Lord would make it possible for him to do what he had been asked to do.[27]

Elder Benson's experience is not unlike that of all men and women of faith who not only believe that God exists but are striving to believe that He will overrule for their good. Living with faith is not for the faint of heart. Great Britain's Rabbi Lord Jonathan Sacks put it this way: "You read Jane Austen [and] you put it back on the shelf and it makes no further demand of you until you feel like reading it again. But you read a sacred text and you put it back on the shelf [and] it's still making a demand of you hours later, days later, weeks later. It is saying this is a truth to be lived. . . . That is the difference between religion and culture. . . . Unless you hear a command [or] an obligation that comes from beyond you, you will not be able to generate sustainable, [actionable faith]."[28]

As Elder Benson and the Saints of Europe found, the greater one's faith, the greater one's hope—for courage, for better days, for help from the Lord, and for the privilege eventually of dwelling "with God in a state of never-ending happiness" (Mosiah 2:41). "Wherefore, if a man have faith he must needs have hope" (Moroni 7:42).

Elder Neal A. Maxwell taught that "in the geometry of restored theology, hope has a greater circumference than faith. If faith increases, the perimeter of hope stretches correspondingly. Just as doubt, despair, and desensitization go together, so do faith, hope, and charity. The latter, however, must be carefully and constantly nurtured, whereas despair, like dandelions, needs so little encouragement to sprout and spread."[29]

There are times when life is difficult enough, for whatever reasons, that it's all we can do to exercise even "a particle of faith." Sometimes we can't do much more than "desire to believe" (Alma 32:27). And yet the promise is that even in times of weakness—perhaps particularly in times of weakness—if we'll let the desire to believe work within us, and have faith in God and in His promises, then the Spirit will manifest truth to us, and it will begin to take root and grow (see Alma 32:27–30).

Thus I repeat: Even the thorniest questions we have about unfulfilled dreams, or unanswered personal prayers, or the doctrinal foundation of the Church's position on complex issues, or moments in Church history that seem confusing, are actually opportunities to receive personal revelation, gain knowledge, and increase in faith.

There are some things that covenant men and women need to be willing to accept in faith. This is the case because it is dangerous, if not impossible, for mortal minds to attempt to articulate or even understand omniscience.

Jacob was saying something about the Lord's omniscience when he declared, "How unsearchable are the depths of the mysteries of him; and it is impossible that man should find out all his ways. And no man knoweth of his ways save it be revealed unto him; wherefore, . . . despise not the revelations of God." He continued, declaring simply, "Seek not to counsel the Lord, but to take counsel from his hand" (Jacob 4:8, 10).

It is difficult for us to comprehend God, let alone think like Him. "For as the heavens are higher than the earth, so are my ways higher than your ways, and my thoughts than your thoughts" (Isaiah 55:9).

God the Father and His Son Jesus Christ are both omniscient and omnipotent. They understand everything and know everything including understanding us and the complexities of mortality perfectly. Further, all things are before Them—meaning, They see the end from the beginning. In short, They know things we don't know and see things we don't see. They know us perfectly, understand perfectly the path we are on, and judge and rule with perfect mercy, justice, and grace.

We live in an imperfect world, surrounded by imperfect people, and we must deal constantly with our own imperfections. And, said

President Gordon B. Hinckley, we also live in "an age of pessimism." That pessimism is manifest in the kinds of criticism (both personal and institutional) that now circle the globe in seconds through social media, in deteriorating moral norms, and in the range of philosophies that are propagated in sound bites. But President Hinckley put such pessimistic practices in their place when he then declared that "ours is a mission of faith. To my brethren and sisters everywhere, I call upon you to reaffirm your faith, to move this work forward across the world. You can make it stronger by the manner in which you live. Let the gospel be your sword and your shield."[30]

In other words, it takes a wrestle. But the reward for engaging in that wrestle is the magnificent gift of increasing faith in our Father and in His Son.

CHAPTER 5

CHERISHING KEYS

I recently underwent a knee-replacement operation, generally considered the most difficult joint replacement from which to recover. I can't speak to that comparison, but I can join the chorus of recovering knee patients who admit that rehab is tough. It takes a long time, and it hurts.

As is typically the case with adversity, I've learned some things during this process, two of which I'll mention. The first was highlighted by a statement stenciled on the wall of the rehab center I frequented for several weeks: "Don't worry about perfection. Worry about progress." It turns out that this declaration is not only true for a recovering knee patient, it's true for mortality as well.

Though perfection is our ultimate objective and destination, it is not something that will occur here and not something we earn. Ultimately, perfection will be a gift from our Father. So fixating on perfection during mortality can become an immobilizing distraction. Progress, however, is another thing entirely. We can make progress in countless ways, large and small, every day of our lives if we choose to. During rehab, I was reminded how motivating it is to experience even the tiniest progress.

The first time I went to rehab, I couldn't bend my knee very far, couldn't straighten it out, couldn't even lift it up off of the training table. But as I began to do the prescribed exercises, all of that began to change—slowly but steadily. With each visit, I could bend the knee a little further, straighten it a little more, and endure more strenuous exercises. Rehab was painful, but it was also surprisingly motivating. Though I would leave feeling tired and sore, I often felt a real sense of accomplishment—even moments of jubilation—because I could do more than I'd done the last time. There was progress, and it felt *so* encouraging!

Our spirits *want* to progress. When we're making progress, even a little, we feel better about ourselves. If we aren't progressing, we can't buy enough or entertain ourselves enough or work hard enough or even medicate ourselves enough to feel good about our lives.

On my very first visit to rehab, my physical therapist told me that she didn't want to see me limp again. I said, "You're kidding, right? Just a few days ago a surgeon cut my leg in two places, lifted out a knee, and inserted a foreign object that, at this point, my leg doesn't like very much. I'm barely getting around on a crutch. But you don't want me to limp?"

Her matter-of-fact response caught my attention: "No. I don't want you to limp any longer. Limping is a habit, and I don't want you to get used to walking that way. Don't limp." She gave that instruction with such finality that I thought about it every time I walked. It seemed crazy at first, but her insistence that I rise above what seemed normal at that point helped me walk much better, much faster than I would have. Sometimes habits we think are defensible and explainable are really excuses to keep from progressing.

A second learning from rehab is that we typically need help to progress. During this grueling process, friends and family did things for me I simply could not do myself. I would not have survived the first few weeks without them. But there was one person who gave a distinctive kind of help that no one else could duplicate: my physical therapist.

Her help was unique, for several reasons: First, she could see the path ahead and knew what awaited me; second, she had training that authorized her to prescribe a regimen that would make me stronger; third, she could warn me about pitfalls and tell me how to avoid them; fourth, she was able to help me get back on the path when I had a setback, usually of my own making; and finally, she cheered me on. Her encouragement spoke to me differently than anyone else's because she spoke with credibility.

When she said, "You're walking better," it made me want to work harder to do even better next time. I quickly saw that my physical therapist knew what she was talking about and that I could trust her to lead me through the grueling process of rehab.

This was my first experience with rehab. But aren't we all in the midst of a kind of rehabilitation: a spiritual rehabilitation? Our challenge is to put off the natural man, yield to the enticings of the Holy Spirit, and become saints through the Atonement of Jesus Christ (see Mosiah 3:19). This process is rehabilitative by nature. And we need help through it.

Thankfully, gratefully, we have help—help that's even better than a skilled and compassionate physical therapist. The Lord has given us prophets, seers, and revelators who see the path ahead; who have authority and power that authorize them to prescribe a spiritual regimen designed to help us get stronger; who warn us about pitfalls and setbacks and how to avoid them; who, when we have setbacks, often of our own making, show us how to heal; and who cheer us on by speaking in the name of the Lord and communicating His love for us.

How important are the Lord's prophets to us? And how important are they to the Lord? One of the major, recurring messages of the Book of Mormon is that the Lord repeatedly sends prophets to the earth to help those who will listen. Three examples will suffice:

First, as Lehi prepared to die, he spoke to each of his sons. He promised Laman and Lemuel that if they would follow Nephi, they would retain their "first blessing," or birthright, but if they didn't, they would not.

Among Lehi's last words were his warnings about following the prophet—their younger brother Nephi (see 2 Nephi 1:28–32).

Second, the Lord repeatedly sent prophets to the Jaredites, warning them that because of their wickedness and idolatry they would be destroyed if they did not repent. But the Jaredites repeatedly rejected the prophets: "And it came to pass that the people did revile against the prophets, and did mock them" (Ether 7:24; see also 11:2). The Jaredite civilization was destroyed, at least in part because they rejected and cast out prophets.

Third, when the Savior was crucified, there was widespread destruction in the New World. Nephi foresaw this, prophesying almost six hundred years earlier that the Savior's death would be a "great and terrible" day for the wicked, who would "perish because they cast out the prophets, . . . and stone them" (2 Nephi 26:3). He also promised that the righteous who hearkened to the words of the prophets would not be destroyed (see v. 8).

In fulfillment of prophecy, at the time of the Crucifixion, the city of Moroni sank into the sea. Moronihah was buried. Zarahemla burned. And dozens of other cities were destroyed: "And behold, the city of Laman, and the city of Josh, and the city of Gad, and the city of Kishkumen, have I caused to be burned with fire, and the inhabitants thereof, because of their wickedness in casting out the prophets, and stoning those whom I did send to declare unto them concerning their wickedness and their abominations."

The record explains that these catastrophic events occurred "because they did cast them all out, that there were none righteous among them, I did send down fire and destroy them, that their wickedness and abominations might be hid from before my face, that the blood of the prophets and the saints whom I sent among them might not cry unto me from the ground against them" (3 Nephi 9:10–11).

It seems like a low bar, to be allowed to live just because you don't cast out and stone the prophets. And yet many Nephites and Lamanites couldn't pass that simple test. The tragic events in the New World at the time of the Crucifixion occurred because the people rejected the Lord's prophets.

Samuel the Lamanite delivered a stinging rebuke of the Nephites for rejecting prophets in favor of self-appointed leaders who condoned their sins: "O ye wicked and ye perverse generation; . . . how long will ye suffer yourselves to be led by foolish and blind guides? Yea, how long will ye choose darkness rather than light?" (Helaman 13:29).

In all ages, there have been and are penalties and consequences for rejecting the Lord's anointed, as He explained to Joseph Smith: "And the day cometh that they who will not hear the voice of the Lord, neither the voice of his servants, neither give heed to the words of the prophets and apostles, shall be cut off from among the people" (D&C 1:14).

The Lord's frequent, repeated warnings about listening to His prophets raise the question: What does stoning and casting out prophets, seers, and revelators look like today? Avoiding their messages? Criticizing them? Suggesting they step aside when the vicissitudes of age overtake them? Using social media to attack them? Leaking records or videos of private meetings in an effort to embarrass them? Attempting to discredit them? Or simply refusing to listen to them? The list could go on and on.

If we don't listen to prophets, seers, and revelators, it's the same as not having prophets, seers, and revelators.

Not long ago I attended a devotional in a young adult stake where members of the stake were encouraged to bring every question they had about marriage, including the Church's position on gay marriage. It was a remarkable evening. The questions were thoughtful, poignant, and pointed, and they covered one sensitive issue after another. The stake presidency responded in a direct, confident, but humble manner. If they didn't know the answers, they said so. Often their responses directed those present to the scriptures and invited them to study more deeply on their own.

For me, though, the highlight of the evening came in the stake president's concluding remarks. In response to a question from someone experiencing same-sex attraction who was frustrated by the Church's position on gay marriage, the stake president responded, "Please understand that Satan will do everything he can to encourage you to separate yourself from those who hold priesthood keys. My plea is that, regardless of the nature of your personal struggles, you don't ever succumb to that temptation. Those who hold keys can help you and guide you in ways others cannot."

In that brief statement, the stake president put in perspective the profound privilege we have of being led, on all levels of Church government, by those who have priesthood keys—which keys open the flow of God's power to all who serve and labor under their direction. This applies in a unique way to prophets, seers, and revelators, who hold *all* of the keys of the kingdom of God.

Understanding the foundational doctrine that a living prophet and living apostles walk the earth today is crucial to understanding the unique nature of The Church of Jesus Christ of Latter-day Saints. The truth about prophets does not depend upon the votes of men and women, nor is it based upon reason, intellect, or popularity. The Lord's Church is led by His living prophet, who becomes President of the Church through a process put in place by the Lord Himself.

The Lord is the prophets' schoolmaster. Some years prior to becoming President of the Church, President Gordon B. Hinckley declared: "There isn't any doubt in my mind that the man who becomes the President of the Church is schooled and disciplined by the Lord over a long period of time for this responsibility. In that process his individuality is not blurred; rather it is sharpened. The Lord trains a man and disciplines him. He tests his heart and his substance. And in a natural process that He directs, He moves through the Quorum of the Twelve a man to become the senior apostle who on the death of the President becomes the President of the Church. There is no campaigning but only the quiet operation of a divine plan that provides inspired and tested leadership. The Lord is at the helm of this work, and the President of the Church is an instrument in His hands to carry forward this work and to strengthen His kingdom."[31]

Does having this divinely inspired structure in place mean mistakes are never made in the Lord's Church? Of course not. The Lord runs His Church with mortals, and sometimes mortals make mistakes. As Elder Jeffrey R. Holland explained, "Except in the case of His only perfect Begotten Son, imperfect people are all God has ever had to work with. That must be terribly frustrating to Him, but He deals with it. So should we. And when you see imperfection, remember that the limitation is *not* in the divinity of the work."[32]

Moroni articulated the most productive way to respond to mortal errors when he admonished future readers of the Book of Mormon that "whoso receiveth this record, and shall not condemn it because of the imperfections which are in it, the same shall know of greater things than these" (Mormon 8:12). Moroni's promise is simple but profound: Those who aren't derailed by mortal imperfections but who see the truth in this divine book of scripture will be given to know and understand more. Likewise, those who see the divinity in the Lord's organization and are not derailed by the imperfections of the Lord's servants place themselves in a position to hear the voice of the Lord through them.

President Dieter F. Uchtdorf testified that as "one who has seen first-hand the councils and workings of this Church, I bear solemn witness that no decision of significance affecting this Church or its members is ever made without earnestly seeking the inspiration, guidance, and approbation of our Eternal Father. This is the Church of Jesus Christ. God will not allow His Church to drift from its appointed course or fail to fulfill its divine destiny."[33]

No other men on earth have had the kind of preparation members of the First Presidency and Quorum of the Twelve have had. Are they infallible? No. But are they unique in all the world? Absolutely.

I have had a wide range of experiences with the senior leaders of the Church. Both Church and professional assignments have created reasons to meet with them countless times over several decades now. My experiences have run the gamut. I have received priesthood blessings from some, been chastised by others, and experienced many things in between those extremes. But I cannot recall a time I've been in a room where a prophet, seer, and revelator was present that the Spirit did not remind me in whose presence I was.

These are not perfect men. Nor would they want us to think of them that way. They are experiencing mortality just as we are, and they have their own weaknesses and strengths with which to deal. But they are the most unflawed group of leaders on earth. Their mission is to help the

Father accomplish His mission, which is to bring to pass the immortality and eternal life of each of us (see Moses 1:39). Thus their motives are unencumbered by any longing for personal gain or popularity.

When all is said and done, there is nothing in this for them—at least, not in the way the world measures success. No fame, no celebrity, no wealth, and no worldly power. To the contrary, they are under constant scrutiny. And as the world becomes more wicked, and they remain dutybound by the nature of their sacred ordination to defend and uphold truth, the criticism and scrutiny they bear will only intensify.

Most important, there are fifteen men—and fifteen only—whom the Lord has entrusted with *all priesthood keys*. No other leaders anywhere can compare.

No wonder our Father and His Son plead with us to listen to them. To pay strict heed to what prophets, seers, and revelators have to say. And to *cherish* the power and direction that flow through those keys.

A few years ago, while I was teaching institute, one student taught me and our entire class an invaluable lesson. It was the week following general conference, and we were sharing what we had heard, learned, and felt. A young woman raised her hand and said that she had received more answers to personal questions during that general conference than any other and believed it was because of the way she had prepared for it. Six months earlier, she and a friend had decided they would read or listen to a general conference address every day. "I believe that because the Lord could see I had taken the words of His prophets seriously from the last conference," she said, "He gave me even more personal inspiration during *this* general conference."

Perhaps one of the greatest things we could do for rising generations and for our families would be to encourage them to gain *their own witness* that prophets, seers, and revelators walk the earth. All who have a testimony of their divine call are in a position to benefit from the keys they bear. Prophets and apostles are able to show us the way ahead, to use the authority of their keys to guide us and help us grow spiritually stronger, to warn us about pitfalls and setbacks, to help us heal when we stumble, and to cheer us on.

If we have the Lord's prophet and apostles, we have everything. If we don't, The Church of Jesus Christ of Latter-day Saints is no different from any other organization. My witness is that Joseph Smith saw what he said he saw in that grove of trees in upstate New York, and that he and all who have succeeded him are prophets in every sense of the word.

The Lord's prophet walks the earth today. The contrast between the leadership of prophets of God and the leadership of the world will continue to become increasingly stark. At times, we may have to wrestle to understand and to accept our leaders' counsel. But the only safety for the days ahead lies in following the prophet.

CHAPTER 6

STANDING AS WITNESSES

I have a treasured friend, not of our faith, whom I met some years ago when we were both serving as members of a White House Commission to the United Nations. I knew practically nothing about that environment, whereas she not only knew the ropes but had the respect of delegates globally. She basically took me under her wing and mentored me through that experience. I have tremendous respect for her and the work she has done to strengthen and protect youth and families worldwide.

Not long ago, my friend had an assignment that brought her in and out of Salt Lake City for a period of time. As it turned out, she was in the city the weekend of the general women's session of general conference, though I didn't realize it at the time. A mutual friend did, however, and offered her a ticket to the meeting. And she went.

Not long thereafter, we had lunch together, and during our conversation she mentioned that she had enjoyed attending the general women's meeting and was still thinking about what she had observed there. I asked what had caught her attention, and she replied, "Well, there were four things. Let me tell you what they are, in ascending order of importance.

"First," she said, "everyone from the ushers to the women sitting next to me were so friendly. I felt very welcome."

She continued, "Second, I was fascinated that every woman was wearing a dress. When I asked those around me why everyone was in Sunday dress on a Saturday evening, they responded, 'We show our love for the Lord by wearing our best when we worship Him.'" She admitted that she couldn't remember the last time she'd gone to church and found every woman in traditional Sunday dress.

"Third, I noticed that every speaker quoted scripture," she said. "I liked that. I wish there were more scripture taught in my church."

Then she said something unforgettable. "What struck me the most, though, was that everyone who spoke said 'I witness,' or something like that. What was it that they said?" she asked, looking at me for an explanation. I responded that, yes, everyone who spoke witnessed, or bore testimony, about what they know to be true. "I was quite taken with that," she said, "that everyone was willing to declare with confidence what they know to be true."

I was struck by the fact that she was so affected by the bearing of testimony—something so very characteristic of the privilege of being a Latter-day Saint.

Consider the miracle of it! Through the power of the Holy Ghost, *we can know what is true and what is not.* We can know what is true *with enough confidence* that we can testify of it.

We can bear witness only of what we *know.* We cannot testify of a wish or a hope or a belief. We can *express* a hope, a wish, or a belief. But we cannot stand as witnesses of Jesus Christ unless we can bear witness of Him. We can defend the faith only if we *have* faith.

Gratefully, we don't have to understand everything to receive a witness.

We don't have to know everything to receive a witness.

We don't have to be called to positions of leadership to receive a witness.

We don't have to have answers to every question to receive a witness.

But we must *receive* a witness before we can *bear* witness and before we can *stand* as a witness.

As the world marches steadily toward the Second Coming, fewer and fewer people will be in a position or will be willing to declare their faith. So the bearing of testimony will become an even greater distinction and a light in the darkness to those whose spirits are receptive to the truth. As it is, society and popular culture seem determined to set aside any semblance of faith or right and wrong—hence the centuries-old discussion about moral relativism, which has been debated from ancient Greece until the present day. But the world's condition in the twenty-first century comes as no surprise to the Lord, who told the Prophet Joseph Smith that we are living in the "eleventh hour," that this is the last time He will call laborers into His vineyard, and that His "vineyard has become corrupted every whit" (D&C 33:3–4).

But the Lord also declared that in the midst of all this moral and spiritual chaos, the fulness of His gospel would be "proclaimed by the weak and the simple unto the ends of the world" (D&C 1:23). And He promised that if we would open our mouths, they would be filled (see D&C 33:8–9).

You and I are the "weak and the simple," but we are not here now by accident or without the Lord's endorsement. Make no mistake about it: We are here now because in the beginning our Father *chose* us to be here now. And He has hard work for us to do. Part of that hard work comes in dealing with a world that is discarding religion wholesale, that in large measure no longer believes in truth.

There are at least two different ways to think about truth. President Spencer W. Kimball taught that "there are relative truths, and there are also absolute truths which are the same yesterday, today, and forever—never changing. These absolute truths are not altered by the opinions of men."[34] There are instances in which only the Spirit can help us differentiate between the two. Consider Nephi, taught from childhood that he should not kill, being commanded by the Lord to take Laban's life so that a nation would not "dwindle and perish in unbelief" (1 Nephi 4:13).

On the other hand, the truth is that there are absolute truths, one of which is that God the Father and His doctrine are unchanging. Said President Kimball: "Even though individuals may fall, the Church and the gospel are here to stay, and all the powers of the earth and hell cannot effect total apostasy again. . . . [The Church] is the 'only true and living church' that is fully recognized with the authority to perform for him, and the only one with a total and comprehensive and true program which will carry men to powers unbelievable and to realms incredible. *This is an absolute truth.* It cannot be disproved. . . . Most of the world disbelieves it, ministers attempt to disprove it, intellectuals think to rationalize it out of existence; but when all the people of the world are dead, and . . . the highly trained are mouldering in their graves, the truth will go forward—the Church will continue triumphant and the gospel will still be true."[35]

Absolute truths are taught and confirmed by the Spirit. They do not change based upon commentators, polls, journalists, the opinions of man, or the number of people who agree that they are true.

David Brooks, a cultural and political columnist for the *New York Times*, wrote about the strength and contribution of religions that dare to declare truth: "Vague, uplifting, nondoctrinal religiosity doesn't actually last. The religions that grow, succor, and motivate people to perform heroic acts of service are usually theologically rigorous, arduous in practice and definite in their convictions about what is True and what is False. That's because people are not gods. No matter how special some individuals may think they are, they don't have the ability to understand the world on their own, establish rules of good conduct on their own, or avoid the temptations of laziness on their own. The religions that thrive have exactly what 'The Book of Mormon' [musical] ridicules: communal theologies, doctrines and codes of conduct rooted in claims of absolute truth."[36]

In response to journalists who routinely asked how it was that the Church continued to grow when many other religions were losing adherents, President Gordon B. Hinckley said much the same thing: "The Church is a constant in a world of change. It is an anchor in a world of shifting values."[37]

Consider, then, not just the advantage but the miracle of being able to know the answers to some of life's greatest imponderables and to feel confident that they are true. Think what it means to know who we are, why we are here, what we are expected to accomplish while here, where we're going, and how to enter and stay on the path that leads ultimately to something much greater than anything this life has to offer. And contemplate the unspeakable privilege of having direct access to God's power through the Holy Ghost, the priesthood, the temple, prophets, and so on.

This is not to say that members of

The Church of Jesus Christ of Latter-day Saints know everything, because we don't. We believe in continuing revelation. There is more to come on many subjects. But as we search the scriptures, follow the prophet, worship in the temple, pray with sincere intent, and seek earnestly, we have the privilege of engaging in a spiritual wrestle and learning as much as we're willing to pay the price to know.

President Gordon B. Hinckley put the importance of knowing for ourselves—*and the responsibility attached to it*—in context when he declared that "ours is a vision greater than that granted any other people who have walked the earth. It encompasses all of the sons and daughters of God in all generations of time. . . . No other people in any other dispensation have ever had so great a responsibility. It is the truth of the everlasting gospel that will save us. It is teaching those truths, and making them effective in the lives of people everywhere, that must become and ever be our consuming mission."[38]

I attended an event not long ago where Elder Quentin L. Cook spoke to an audience filled with men and women who have devoted their lives to serving the Lord. It would be impossible to calculate the breadth and depth of service that particular group has rendered as General Authorities, general officers, and priesthood and auxiliary leaders on every level. On the face of it, you wouldn't think those people needed motivation to testify of truth. And yet, that night Elder Cook told us that we needed to do two things much better: defend the Prophet Joseph Smith and bear witness that Jesus is the Christ.

Elder Cook didn't stop there. He brought with him a white-gloved archivist from the Church History Library who displayed two intriguing artifacts: an original manuscript page of the Book of Mormon and a journal written in Joseph Smith's hand.

I had seen pages from the original Book of Mormon manuscript before, but this time something struck me—probably because the manuscript page was displayed side by side with the journal, which was open to an entry Joseph had made. The journal page had many changes—words crossed out, insertions, and so on—but there wasn't a single word changed on that long page of Book of Mormon manuscript. Not one.

That caught my attention. I've been in the publishing business for almost forty years and have worked with *many* of the most spiritually gifted men and women in our culture: inspired leaders, thinkers, writers, and speakers. In all these years, one thing I have rarely seen is a page of manuscript with no changes. I have had authors tell me their words are perfect as they roll forth from their laptops, but they almost never are. It is much more typical for even the most gifted writers to write and rewrite ad nauseam. And yet, that evening I was looking at an unchanged manuscript page recorded by a scribe as Joseph translated the Book of Mormon by inspiration.

Speaking at the Library of Congress, Elder D. Todd Christofferson put a fine point on the nature of this accomplishment: "Joseph dictated the entire 250,000-word, 600-page manuscript in some 65 working days between April and June 1829. This was done in a single draft with very few strikeouts or corrections. It is an especially remarkable feat given Joseph's educational background."[39]

Speaking as a publisher, I don't believe that *any* man could have written *one draft* containing page after page of unaltered Book of Mormon manuscript, a manuscript filled with intricate geographical and cultural descriptions, a cast of thousands, and soaring doctrine much of it unknown at the time—in less than ninety days. It's just not possible—especially by an unskilled writer who, according to his wife (who also doubled as a scribe at times), "could neither write nor dictate a coherent and well-worded letter, let alone dictate a book like the Book of Mormon."[40]

Emma Smith later told her son: "My belief is that the Book of Mormon is of divine authenticity—I have not the slightest doubt of it. I am satisfied that no man could have dictated the writing of the manuscripts unless he was inspired, for, when acting as his scribe, your father would dictate to me hour after hour; and when returning after meals or after interruptions, he would at once begin where he had left off, without either seeing the manuscript or having any portion of it read to him. This was a usual thing for him to do. It would have been improbable that a learned man could do this and for one so ignorant and unlearned as he was, it was simply impossible."[41]

Now, I realize there have actually been a number of changes made to the original Book of Mormon translation. Mormon accounted for such changes when he said in his preface that "if there are faults they are the mistakes of men; wherefore, condemn not the things of God, that ye may be found spotless at the judgment-seat of Christ."[42] Nonetheless, the contrast between a page of text translated through revelation by the Prophet Joseph Smith and a page he wrote of his own accord was striking. For me, it was a piece of "evidence" supporting the Prophet's account of the coming forth of the Book of Mormon.

My witness of that sacred book, however, is not based on seeing unaltered manuscript pages. A spiritual witness is never based on tangible evidence. A witness of truth comes only as the Holy Ghost speaks to our minds *and* to our hearts (see D&C 8:2–3). The Spirit is the only witness that is ultimately irrefutable.

When the Spirit bears witness of truth, we have a sacred obligation to share that light and knowledge. Said Elder Neil L. Andersen, "As evil increases in the world, there is a compensatory spiritual power for the righteous. As the world slides from its spiritual moorings, the Lord prepares the way for those who seek Him, offering them greater assurance, greater confirmation, and greater confidence in the spiritual direction they are traveling. The gift of the Holy Ghost becomes a brighter light in the emerging twilight."[43]

President Henry B. Eyring underscored this truth when he dedicated the remodeled Deseret

Book Company corporate office in May 2009. As he shared a vision of the impact that organization could have throughout the world, he concluded with this statement: "The increasing darkness in the world will be your opportunity."

Surely this prophecy, this statement of truth, applies with even more far-reaching implications to the Church and its covenant-keeping members. The increasing darkness in the world *will be* an opportunity for all who are prepared to teach and proclaim truth and who come to know for themselves what the Book of Mormon character Sherem came to know—though, hopefully, under less tragic circumstances.

Sherem was learned, articulate, and charismatic. He was also an anti Christ who used every trick in the book, including his "perfect knowledge of the language of the people," to deceive and distort the truth and to "lead away the hearts of the people" into Satan's entanglements. Unfortunately, many fell for his tactics.

Sherem wasn't satisfied with deceiving the general populace, however; he was intent on shaking Jacob from his faith. He badgered Jacob, debated with Jacob, and taunted Jacob to show him a sign of God's power (see Jacob 7:1–13).

Jacob's response was classic, not to mention brilliant: "What am I that I should tempt God to show unto thee a sign in the thing which thou knowest to be true? Yet thou wilt deny it, because thou art of the devil. Nevertheless, not my will be done; *but if God shall smite thee*, let that be a sign unto thee that he has power, both in heaven and in earth." Sherem obviously didn't expect that the sign he insisted on seeing would be devastating for him. But with Jacob's words, Sherem was struck to the earth and had to be "nourished for the space of many days" (Jacob 7:14–15; emphasis added).

We don't know exactly what happened to Sherem during his incapacitation. But he evidently had some kind of conversion experience, because the time came when he announced that he would soon die and that he wanted to speak to the people before he did.

What Sherem declared is both surprising and instructive. First, he spoke plainly to the people and "denied the things which he had taught them." And then, he testified of three things: he "confessed the Christ, and the power of the Holy Ghost, and the ministering of angels" (Jacob 7:17).

Imagine, of all the things he could have said to the people he had tried to deceive, he bore witness of three fundamental ways we gain access to the knowledge and power of God: through Jesus Christ and His Atonement, through the ministering of the Holy Ghost, and through the ministering of angels.

Receiving a witness enables us to bear witness. And bearing witness can have profound results.

A few years ago, a reporter from an international broadcasting network visited Salt Lake City to research a story on women in the Church. I liked this reporter. She'd done her homework and asked intelligent questions. Inevitably, however, the conversation turned to a predictable question: "How do you feel about not being eligible for priesthood ordination?"

Because of her respectful demeanor, and because she seemed to sincerely want to understand the privileges women in the Church have, I found myself explaining more than I would have otherwise—particularly about the ways that women have direct access to the power of God. Although I could say little about the temple, I did tell her that as a woman endowed with power in the temple, I had access to God's power—or priesthood power—for my own life. And I explained that *my* focus had long been on learning how to gain full access to that power.

That statement stopped her. She leaned back in her chair, paused, and then asked: "Are you saying that you believe *you* have more access to God's power than I do?"

What a loaded question from a journalist! My brain began to spin in search of a truthful but politically correct response. But for some reason, that day I could not bring myself to soft-pedal the answer and in the process sell our doctrine or our privileges as women short. So finally I said, "Well, actually . . . yes."

"Now, do *not* misunderstand what I'm saying," I quickly added. "I am *not* saying the Lord loves me more than He loves you or that I'm better than you. I am not saying that He is more likely to bless me than He is you. I am not suggesting any of those things. But if you're asking if I believe I have greater access to God's power than you do, then the answer has to be yes. That is one of the blessings of joining this Church. We believe that when we make promises to God to follow His Son, He in turn makes promises to us. And one of those promises is that He will give us greater access to His power."

Though I was nervous about the answer spilling out of my heart and mouth, I couldn't deny what was happening. The Spirit filled the room and disarmed the reporter. Her demeanor softened, and then she asked if I could describe how the gospel affects me personally. In other words, she opened the door for me to testify.

Among other things, I told her that Jesus Christ hasn't just made a difference in my life, that He and His gospel have made *all* the difference. I explained that I have experienced the Savior's healing, strengthening power again and again. And I testified that every good thing that has ever happened to me has come *because* of my membership in His Church.

At that point, the Spirit *flooded* the room and we were both in tears. After she regained her composure, she said, "That is beautiful." That day I experienced the sublime beauty of standing as a witness and bearing witness of truth.

That day I was reminded that when we testify of truth, the Spirit bears witness. Every time. And I also felt a simple confirmation of a profound truth: *There are divine laws that govern access to God's power.* And men and women who make covenants with God, and who keep those covenants, have greater access to that power. It is as Alma taught, that those who enter into covenants with the Lord become eligible to have Him "pour out his Spirit more abundantly" upon them (Mosiah 18:10). No wonder Nephi foresaw that those who would seek to bring forth Zion in our day would be blessed with "the gift and the power of the Holy Ghost" (1 Nephi 13:37).

In short, we can either live our lives alone, relying largely upon our own strengths, or we can live them with the help of heaven. How much help we receive from Above is largely up to us. None of us are talented enough, smart enough, wise enough, or resilient enough to do the work of building the kingdom—and to become the men and women we have the potential of becoming—without the help of heaven.

A friend who teaches preschool related a conversation she had with a boy in her preschool class. From the beginning of the school year, this teacher noticed how kind this boy was. He was "all boy" during recess, but kind and considerate to everyone in the classroom. One day she pulled him aside and said, "Brandon, you are such a good member of this class. Why are you so kind to everyone?"

His immediate response was matter-of-fact: "Because Jesus has rules."

Trying to contain her grin, the teacher probed further. "What does that mean?"

He responded without hesitating: "If we want Jesus to help us, we have to follow His rules."

My friend concluded, "There you have it, the secret of a great life reduced to two sentences by a four-year-old."

Obedience to the Savior's "rules" opens the heavens and blesses us with a witness that Jesus Christ is exactly who prophets and apostles testify that He is and that He indeed "rose again the third day."[44]

According to Elder Bruce R. McConkie, "The Atonement of Christ is the most basic and fundamental doctrine of the gospel, and it is the *least understood of all our revealed truths*. Many of us have a superficial knowledge and rely upon the Lord and His goodness to see us through the trials and perils of life. But if we are to have faith like that of Enoch and Elijah, we must believe what they believed, know what they knew, and live as they lived."[45]

What happens to us when we understand what the Savior did for us? I recently met a young mother in the middle of a painful divorce who told me that, as difficult as it was, she was growing spiritually in a way she'd never experienced. "I had always known that if I repented, the Lord would forgive me," she said. "But I did not realize that the Atonement could *heal* me of my sadness and mistakes. This is the first time I've realized that He has power to heal my heart."

Some decades ago, I experienced a crushing emotional blow that left me adrift in a sea of hurt and loneliness. I didn't handle myself very well during that painful season. I flailed about emotionally and wallowed in anger, including at the Lord for "letting me down." In the midst of that ordeal, however, I received a priesthood blessing in which I was told that this trial was a "gift." At the time, I couldn't comprehend how that could be true.

But I wrestled for understanding and for peace. Neither came quickly. During the process, however, I began to understand for the first time that the Atonement, as Elder Bruce C. Hafen taught, was not just for sinners.[46] Because the Lord took upon Himself our sins, weaknesses, mistakes, and agonies, there is godly power available to help His followers deal with all kinds of pain.

That "gift" from many years ago altered the trajectory of my life. For the first time, I understood what Malachi and Nephi meant when they prophesied that the Savior would rise "with healing in his wings" (Malachi 4:2; 2 Nephi 25:13). I appreciated Isaiah's prophecy that He would give those who mourn in Zion "beauty for ashes" and the "oil of joy for mourning" (Isaiah 61:3). I believed that the Savior came "to heal the broken-hearted," the "wounded soul" (Luke 4:18; Jacob 2:8), and that He took upon Himself my pain and would "succor," or run to, me (Alma 7:11–12).

Since that time, I have viewed the Atonement as the source of all healing. The Savior will heal us from sin, *if* we repent. He will heal us from weakness, sadness, and loneliness; from hurt, fear, and mistakes; from the emotional and spiritual bruises of attempting to live covenant lives in a spiritually hostile world; from the effects of unfairness, abuse, and the sins of others; from disappointment, a lack of courage, or wavering faith.

As President Howard W. Hunter declared: "Whatever Jesus lays his hands upon lives. If Jesus lays his hands upon a marriage, it lives. If he is allowed to lay his hands upon the family, it lives."[47]

Knowing that we would need and long for healing of all kinds, the Savior extended this soothing invitation: "Will ye not now return unto me, and repent of your sins, and be converted, that I may heal you? . . . Behold, mine arm of mercy is extended towards you, and *whosoever will come, him will I receive*" (3 Nephi 9:13–14; emphasis added). The greatest healing comes to those who repent and are converted.

Thus, the most sure way to gain access to the Savior's healing, strengthening power is to make covenants with Him and then keep them. When Alma's people were being held captive, the Lord "came to them in their afflictions, saying: Lift up your heads and be of good comfort, for I know of the covenant which ye have made unto me; and I will covenant with my people and deliver them out of bondage." He then promised to ease their burdens such that they could not feel them. "And this will I do," the Lord explained, "that ye may stand as witnesses for me hereafter, and that ye may know of a surety that I, the Lord God, do visit my people in their afflictions" (Mosiah 24:13–14).

The most powerful way to gain a witness of the healing power of Jesus Christ is to *experience* His healing power.

Can anyone do justice to the majesty and mission, let alone the Atonement, of Jesus Christ? Does *anyone* have the words or the understanding to fully communicate who the Savior is and what He did for us?

On the other hand, the Holy Ghost can bear witness of Him with such clarity and power that we can know, without question, that Jesus Christ is our Savior.

A couple of years ago, I was meeting with an evangelical friend in Boston the week prior to the week of Easter. As we concluded and pulled out our phones to check calendars for a follow-up meeting, my friend said, "Well, we can't talk next week, that's Holy Week. It will have to be after that."

I made the mistake of asking, "Do you not work at all next week?" He shot me a look I'll never forget, almost as though I were an infidel. I shifted quickly and asked how he and his family planned to observe Holy Week. He described a full slate of activities—some with the family and some at their church. I found myself wondering why we as a people, who look to the Savior as the center of everything we believe and do, don't seem to be as engaged in celebrating Easter as others are.

I hope the reason is that we seek to worship the Lord and make Him the center of our lives *every* week of the year. But I was struck by my friend's devotion to Holy Week and all it represents. What the Savior did for us in the Garden, on Calvary, and in the Garden Tomb ought to mean that much, and more, to all of us—because the Atonement of Jesus Christ stands as the centerpiece of God's plan for His children.

The Prophet Joseph Smith declared that "the fundamental principles of our religion are the testimony of the Apostles and Prophets, concerning Jesus Christ, that He died, was buried, and rose again the third day, and ascended into heaven; and *all other things* which pertain to our religion are only appendages to it."[48]

According to President Russell M. Nelson, that statement from Joseph Smith provided the impetus for the members of the First Presidency and Quorum of the Twelve Apostles to prepare and sign "The Living Christ" as their testimony of Him. That document was their gift to the Lord and His people, testifying of the Savior's divinity, issued to commemorate the two-thousandth anniversary of His birth in mortality, dated January 1, 2000.[49]

Moroni joined a chorus of prophets when he commended us to "seek this Jesus of whom the prophets and apostles have written" (Ether 12:41). This invokes the question: What is different for you and me when we understand what the Savior did for us and when we seek a personal witness that He is *our* Savior? The answer is, *everything.*

Everything changed because of Jesus Christ.

Everything is better because of Him.

Everything about our Father's plan became operable because of Him.

Everything about life is manageable, especially the painful parts, because of Him.

Everything is possible because of Him.

Every heavenly power and privilege is available to us because of Him and His gospel.

The Savior changed everything for all who are willing to make covenants with Him and then keep them.

Without the Savior and His gospel, we would have no hope. No access to any kind of heavenly power. No family that extends beyond the grave and therefore no hope of anything but the emotionally crippling state of eternal singleness. We would have no escape from sin, from our mistakes, or from the binding cords of the devil. We would have no peace. No joy. No happiness. No healing. No resurrection. No possibility of having our spirits and bodies reunited forever. No reunion of the faithful. No possibility of eternal life. No future.

Brigham Young said that, prior to the Restoration of the gospel, the whole of Christian doctrine could be "simmered down . . . into a snuff box. . . . But when I found Mormonism, I found it was higher than I could reach . . . , deeper than I was capable of comprehending, and calculated to expand the mind, and lead mankind from truth to truth, from light to light, from grace to grace, and exalt him . . . to become associated with Gods and the angels."[50]

None of this would be possible without what the Savior chose to do for us in Gethsemane, on Calvary, and in the Tomb.

> *He is risen! He is risen!*
> *Tell it out with joyful voice.*
> *He has burst his three days' prison;*
> *Let the whole wide earth rejoice.*
> *Death is conquered, man is free.*
> *Christ has won the victory.*[51]

Of that victory, I bear my witness. I can stand as a witness of Him because I have received a witness that Jesus is the Christ and that His

Atonement was perfect and infinite. I bear witness that I have personally experienced His healing, strengthening, enabling power again and again.

The gospel of Jesus Christ has been restored to the earth. We, of all people, are witnesses to the winding-up scenes of not only this dispensation but this earth.

The Savior is going to come again, and all who can stand as witnesses of Him have the profound privilege of helping prepare the earth for His return.

May we engage in the wrestle to gain an unflinching witness of Jesus Christ. May we gain a witness so that we can stand as witnesses of Him "at all times and in all things, and in all places" (Mosiah 18:9). May we stand as witnesses and defend the faith because we have experienced the power of having faith in the Savior of the world.

CONCLUSION

WHAT IS WORTH WRESTLING FOR?

I once had the privilege of meeting and interviewing Randall Wallace at his California home. Wallace came to prominence when he received an Academy Award nomination and a Writer's Guild Award for the screenplay to *Braveheart*. He has also written, and in some cases produced, such movies as *Secretariat, Pearl Harbor, The Man in the Iron Mask, We Were Soldiers,* and *Heaven Is for Real.*

I liked Wallace instantly. From Lizard Lick, Tennessee, his unassuming, country-boy, small-town background resonated with me. His family members were devout Baptists, and when he talked about spending twenty or thirty hours a week "going to church" (everything from the Boy Scouts to Sunday meetings), I felt as though I'd met a kindred spirit.

Prior to our interview, I watched the address he gave at the National Prayer Breakfast in 2011 and was struck by the sincerity of his message about the power of prayer. In our conversation, he was neither self-conscious nor self-righteous as he professed his belief in Jesus Christ and the impact the Savior had in his life.

His career, though celebrated now, has had its share of intense ups and downs. At one point, when he faced the possibility of losing just about everything, he said he was determined that if he went down, he would go down fighting for what he believed, "with his flag flying."

When I asked why he had produced and written so many movies about war, his answer reinforced the rest of his story: "I don't think of  them as war movies," he said. "I write love stories. I want to know what a man or woman loves enough to fight for."

Perhaps that sentiment is the very essence of being willing to engage in the wrestle: to demonstrate to ourselves and to the Lord that we care about Him and His gospel enough to fight, or wrestle, to grow in knowledge and in faith.

There are many things that are worth the wrestle.

It is worth wrestling to understand God's power and how He gives us access to it.

It is worth wrestling to have a deepening understanding and

testimony of the grace of the Lord Jesus Christ, His infinite Atonement, and the healing power that can flow through Him to those who believe in Him.

It is worth wrestling to understand priesthood power and how that power operates in the lives of both men and women.

It is worth wrestling to learn the language of revelation and then to seek revelation regularly.

It is worth wrestling to gain a testimony that Joseph Smith was a prophet, and that he was the Lord's instrument who ushered in the dispensation of the fulness of times.

It is worth wrestling to know that the living prophet is the Lord's mouthpiece, His ordained servant who holds and exercises all priesthood keys, and that the members of the First Presidency and Quorum of the Twelve Apostles are prophets, seers, and revelators.

It is worth wrestling to gain a personal witness that the Book of Mormon is the word of God, and that ancient prophets foresaw our day and recorded the doctrine, truths, and spiritual patterns that would help us negotiate the unique challenges of these last days.

It is worth wrestling to understand the gifts that come from the gift of the Holy Ghost, including the availability of spiritual gifts.

It is worth wrestling to understand the ministering of angels and why Elder Jeffrey R. Holland counseled us to "ask for angels to help us"[52] when we are in need of extra courage, strength, peace, and aid.

It is worth wrestling to understand the plan of salvation and why the family as God decreed it is at the center of the plan.

It is worth wrestling to understand the distinctive gifts and divine endowments of both women and men as well as the unique and vital contributions of all in building the kingdom.

It is worth wrestling to understand and learn how to discuss complex social issues where our doctrine and society's views differ widely, and to do so in a spirit of cooperation and kindness but also candor.

It is worth wrestling to understand how to keep the covenants we have made while living peacefully in a world that increasingly rejects truth and condemns religious belief and practice as provincial, parochial, and in some cases even dangerous.

It is worth wrestling to understand how to live as men and women of God.

It is worth wrestling to be willing to ask the right questions, questions such as: "What is Thy will (regardless of the situation we may find ourselves in)? What would Thou have me do? What would Thou have me say? How would Thou have me feel about a circumstance or outcome or desire?" Sometimes accepting the answers to such questions can require a wrestle.

But those willing to engage in a lifelong spiritual wrestle will be able to say, as did the Prophet Joseph Smith, "I am a lover of the cause of Christ."[53]

There is *so* much that I don't yet understand. There are blessings I have pleaded and prayed for that have not yet come.

But I know what I know. And that knowledge has come from wrestling.

I testify that when we seek truth, humbly and sincerely, the Lord responds.

I testify that He wants to teach us His language and to speak to us with increasing clarity.

I testify that there is not anything, or anyone, or any influence that will prevent The Church of Jesus Christ of Latter-day Saints from fulfilling its foreordained mission.

I testify that our Father and His Son are real, that Their power is real, that Their truth is divinely mandated and directed.

And I testify that the wrestle to follow Them, to come to know Them, and to become more like Them is worth everything.

NOTES

1. Thomas S. Monson, "Welcome to Conference," *Ensign*, November 2012.

2. Russell M. Nelson, "A Plea to My Sisters," *Ensign*, November 2015.

3. Sheri L. Dew, *Go Forward with Faith* (1996), 449.

4. Ibid., 485–86.

5. *Teachings of Presidents of the Church: Brigham Young* (1997), 294.

6. Neal A. Maxwell, *Not My Will, but Thine* (1988), 124.

7. Truman G. Madsen, *Defender of the Faith: The B. H. Roberts Story* (1980), 387.

8. Richard G. Scott, *21 Principles: Divine Truths to Help You Live by the Spirit* (2013), 95–96; emphasis added.

9. Spencer W. Kimball, "Absolute Truth," BYU Devotional, 6 September 1977, found at https: //speeches.byu.edu.

10. As an example, the Gospel Topics essays on lds.org provide a wealth of information on some of the most complex doctrinal and historical topics, including the First Vision, plural marriage, race and priesthood, Mother in Heaven,

the translation and historicity of the Book of Abraham, becoming like God, the Book of Mormon and DNA, and so on.

11. *Teachings of Presidents of the Church: Joseph Smith* (2007), 132.

12. Ibid.

13. Ibid., 268.

14. Henry B. Eyring, "Continuing Revelation," *Ensign*, November 2014; emphasis added.

15. Richard G. Scott, "Acquiring Spiritual Knowledge," *Ensign*, November 1993.

16. Jeffrey R. Holland, "'Cast Not Away Therefore Your Confidence,'" BYU Devotional, 2 March 1999, found at https: //speeches.byu.edu.

17. See D&C 50:25: "And again, verily I say unto you, and I say it that you may know the truth, that you may chase darkness from among you."

18. C. S. Lewis, *The Screwtape Letters*, (San Francisco: Harper, 1996), 57.

19. Kevin J Worthen, "'It Is Not Good That . . . Man Should Be Alone,'" BYU Devotional, 5 January 2016, found at https: //speeches.byu.edu.

20. Jeffrey R. Holland, "Place No More for the Enemy of My Soul," *Ensign*, May 2010.

21. Email, Susannah Bingham Buck to author, 18 February 2016.

22. Gordon B. Hinckley, "Stay the Course—Keep the Faith," *Ensign*, November 1995.

23. Dallin H. Oaks, "Opposition in All Things," *Ensign*, May 2016.

24. In Conference Report, October 1963, 108.

25. Jeffrey R. Holland, "Be Not Afraid, Only Believe," Address to Church Educational System Religious Educators, 6 February 2015.

26. Henry B. Eyring, "Spiritual Preparedness: Start Early and Be Steady," *Ensign*, November 2005.

27. See Sheri L. Dew, *Ezra Taft Benson: A Biography* (1987), chapter 12.

28. "The Case for God," BBC Rosh Hashanah program, 6 September 2010.

29. Neal A. Maxwell, "Brightness of Hope," *Ensign*, November 1994.

30. Gordon B. Hinckley, "Stay the Course—Keep the Faith," *Ensign*, November 1995.

31. See Sheri L. Dew, *Go Forward with Faith*, (1996), xvi.

32. Jeffrey R. Holland, "'Lord, I Believe,'" *Ensign*, May 2013.

33. Dieter F. Uchtdorf, "Come, Join with Us," *Ensign*, November 2014.

34. Spencer W. Kimball, "Absolute Truth," BYU Devotional, 6 September 1977; found at https://speeches.byu.edu.

35. Ibid; emphasis added.

36. "Creed or Chaos," *New York Times*, 11 April 2011.

37. Interview with Lawrence Spicer, London News Service, 28 August 1995; as quoted in "Excerpts from Recent Addresses of President Gordon B. Hinckley," *Ensign*, August 1996.

38. Quoted in Jeffrey R. Holland, "Our Consuming Mission," Address to Church Educational System Religious Educators, 5 February 1999.

39. Sarah Jane Weaver, "Elder D. Todd Christofferson Speaks of the Book of Mormon at the Library of Congress," *Church News*, 8 December 2016.

40. "Last Testimony of Sister Emma," *The Saints' Herald* 26, 1 October 1879, 290.

41. Ibid.

42. Title page, Book of Mormon.

43. Neil L. Andersen, "A Compensatory Spiritual Power for the Righteous," BYU Education Week Devotional, 18 August 2015; found at https://speeches.byu.edu.

44. *Teachings of Presidents of the Church: Joseph Smith* (2007), 49.

45. Bruce R. McConkie, *A New Witness for the Articles of Faith* (1985), xv; emphasis added.

46. See Bruce C. Hafen, *The Broken Heart: Applying the Atonement to Life's Experiences* (1989).

47. Howard W. Hunter, "Reading the Scriptures," *Ensign*, November 1979.

48. *Teachings of Presidents of the Church: Joseph Smith* (2007), 49–50; emphasis added. Joseph Smith's statement continued: "But in connection with these, we believe in the gift of the Holy Ghost, the power of faith, the enjoyment of

the spiritual gifts according to the will of God, the restoration of the house of Israel, and the final triumph of truth."

49. Russell M. Nelson to Sheri Dew, 30 December 2016.

50. Leonard J. Arrington, *Brigham Young: American Moses* (1986), 78n72.

51. "He Is Risen," text by Cecil Frances Alexander, *Hymns of The Church of Jesus Christ of Latter-day Saints* (1985), no. 199.

52. Jeffrey R. Holland, "Place No More for the Enemy of My Soul," *Ensign*, May 2010.

53. *Teachings of Presidents of the Church: Joseph Smith* (2007), 352.